Foundations of Sport and Exercise Psychology

Second Edition
Study Guide

Daniel Gould, PhD
University of North Carolina at Greensboro

Robert S. Weinberg, PhD
Miami University

ISBN 0-7360-0159-X

Developmental Editor: Rebecca Crist; **Assistant Editor:** Chris Enstrom; **Copyeditor:** Harbour Hodder; **Permission Manager:** Heather Munson; **Graphic Designer:** Stuart Cartwright; **Graphic Artist:** Kathleen Boudreau-Fuoss; **Cover Designer:** Jack W. Davis; **Photographer (front cover):** Tim De Frisco/De Frisco Photography; **Illustrator:** Roberto Sabas and Mic Greenberg; **Printer:** Versa Press

Printed in the United States of America   10   9   8   7   6   5   4   3   2

Human Kinetics
Web site: www.humankinetics.com

United States: Human Kinetics, P.O. Box 5076, Champaign, IL 61825-5076
800-747-4457
e-mail: humank@hkusa.com

Canada: Human Kinetics, 475 Devonshire Road, Unit 100, Windsor, ON N8Y 2L5
800-465-7301 (in Canada only)
e-mail: hkcan@mnsi.net

Europe: Human Kinetics, Units C2/C3 Wira Business Park, West Park Ring Road, Leeds LS16 6EB, United Kingdom
+44 (0) 113 278 1708
e-mail: hk@hkeurope.com

Australia: Human Kinetics, 57A Price Avenue, Lower Mitcham, South Australia 5062
08 8277 1555
e-mail: liahka@senet.com.au

New Zealand: Human Kinetics, P.O. Box 105-231, Auckland Central
09-523-3462
e-mail: hkp@ihug.co.nz

C O N T E N T S

Chapter 3   Motivation   **23**

Chapter 4   Arousal, Stress, and Anxiety   **29**

Part III   Understanding Sport and Exercise Environments   **37**

Chapter 5   Competition and Cooperation   **39**

Chapter 6   Feedback, Reinforcement, and Intrinsic Motivation   **43**

Chapter 24   Character Development and Sportspersonship   159

TO THE STUDENT

Foundations of Sport and Exercise Psychology introduces you to the field of sport and exercise psychology. This exciting field focuses on the study of human behavior in certain types of situations—namely, sport and exercise settings. It is designed to provide you with information to bridge the gap between research and practice, and to convey some fundamental principles of professional practice. Hence, information in the book will help you become a more effective fitness instructor, physical educator, coach, athlete, athletic medicine specialist, or even a sport psychologist.

Although we have tried to convey the information in the textbook in a clear, concise and practical fashion, the many details and scientific processes presented might be overwhelming and confusing at times if you have had little background in the field. That's why we wrote this Study Guide—to assist you in learning, understanding, and applying the main concepts of each chapter.

We have included a variety of activities to help sport and exercise psychology come to life. It is our hope that through interacting with your classmates, taking and scoring yourself on psychological tests, conducting self-made experiments or case studies, finding information on the Internet, and completing exercises, you will see how important sport and exercise psychology is to our daily lives. We also hope these activities will help vitalize the information in the book and make studying it a fun and rewarding experience.

Sport and exercise psychology is an amazing field with tremendous potential to help participants involved in sport and physical activity perform better and develop psychologically. We hope this Study Guide helps make the science behind this field clear and useful to you. Now, let's get going by better understanding the field itself and its role in helping sport and exercise participants.

KEY TO ICONS

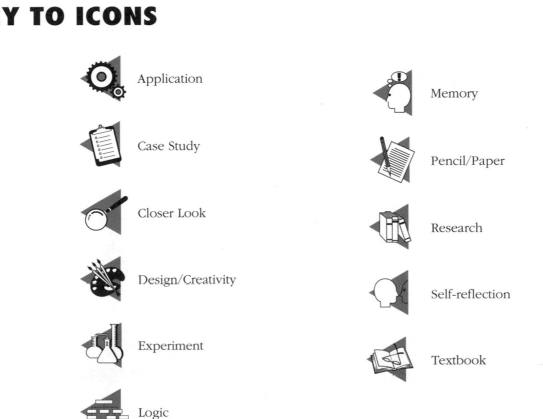

Application

Memory

Case Study

Pencil/Paper

Closer Look

Research

Design/Creativity

Self-reflection

Experiment

Textbook

Logic

ACKNOWLEDGMENTS

The authors would like to thank Kristen Dieffenbach, Christy Greenleaf, and Justine Reel for their invaluable assistance in developing these materials.

CREDITS

Activity 2.3
Adapted, by permission, from R.S. Vealey, 1986, "Conceptualization of sport-confidence and competitive orientation: Preliminary investigation and instrument development," *Journal of Sport Psychology* 8 (3): 244-245.

Graph on page 19
Adapted, by permission, from W.P. Morgan, 1979, Prediction of performance in athletes. In *Coach, athlete, and the sport psychologist*, edited by P. Klavora and J.V. Daniel (Toronto: University of Toronto School of Physical and Health Education), 185.

Activity 4.1, Sport Competition Anxiety Test
Adapted, by permission, from R. Martens, 1977, *Sport competition anxiety test* (Champaign, IL: Human Kinetics), 93.

Activity 4.1, Sport Anxiety Scale
Adapted, by permission, from R.E. Smith, F.L. Smoll, and R.W. Schutz, 1990, "Measurement and correlates of sport-specific cognitive and somatic trait anxiety: The Sport Anxiety Scale," *Anxiety Research* 2: 263-280.

Activity 4.1, State Anxiety Test
Adapted, by permission, from R. Martens, R.S. Vealey, and D. Burton, 1990, *Competitive anxiety in sport* (Champaign, IL: Human Kinetics), 177.

Reward Preference Questionnaire (p. 46)
Adapted by permission, from G.L. Martin and J. Lumsden, 1987, *Coaching: An effective behavioral approach* (St. Louis: Mosby Year Book, Inc.).

Activity 8.1
Adapted, by permission, from A.V. Carron, L.R. Brawley, and W.N. Widmeyer, 1985, "Assessing the cohesion of teams: Validity of the group environmental questionnaire," *Journal of Sport Psychology* 9 (3): 275-294.

Listening Skills Test (p. 72)
Reprinted, by permission, from R. Martens, 1987, *Coaches guide to sport psychology* (Champaign, IL: Human Kinetics), 56.

Box on page 73
Adapted, by permission, from R. Martens, 1987, *Coaches guide to sport psychology* (Champaign, IL: Human Kinetics), 63-64.

Activity 11.1
Adapted, by permission, from R.E. Smith et al., 1994, "Development and validation of a multidimensional measure of sport-specific psychological skills: The Athletic Coping Skills Inventory," *Journal of Sport and Exercise Psychology* 17 (4): 379-398.

Activity 12.1
Adapted, by permission, from T. Orlick, 1986. *Psyching for sport* (Champaign, IL: Human Kinetics), 17-18.

Activity 13.1
Reprinted, by permission, from American Coaching Effectiveness Program, 1987, *Sport psychology*, Level Two (Champaign, IL: Human Kinetics), 74.

Activity 13.2

Reprinted, by permission, from American Coaching Effectiveness Program, 1987, *Sport psychology*, Level Two (Champaign, IL: Human Kinetics), 78.

Activity 13.3

Adapted, by permission, from American Coaching Effectiveness Program, 1987, *Sport psychology*, Level Two (Champaign, IL: Human Kinetics), 69-71.

Activity 14.2

Adapted, by permission, from American Coaching Effectiveness Program, 1987, *Sport psychology*, Level Two (Champaign, IL: Human Kinetics), 140-142.

Activity 15.1

Adapted, by permission, from T. Orlick, 1986, *Psyching for sport* (Champaign, IL: Human Kinetics), 14-16.

Activity 15.3

Adapted, by permission, from American Coaching Effectiveness Program, 1987, *Sport psychology*, Level Two (Champaign, IL: Human Kinetics), 142-143.

Illustration on page 105

Adapted, by permission, from R.S. Weinberg and D. Gould, 1999, *Foundations of sport and exercise psychology*, 2nd ed. (Champaign, IL: Human Kinetics), 313.

Activity 16.1

Adapted, by permission, from American Coaching Effectiveness Program, 1987, *Sport psychology*, Level Two (Champaign, IL: Human Kinetics), 113-114.

Activity 16.2

Adapted, by permission, from American Coaching Effectiveness Program, 1987, *Sport psychology*, Level Two (Champaign, IL: Human Kinetics), 114-115.

Activity 16.3

Reprinted, by permission, American Coaching Effectiveness Program, 1987, *Sport psychology* Level Two (Champaign, IL: Human Kinetics), 131.

Table on page 142

Adapted, by permission, from D. Gould et al., 1996, "Burnout in competitive junior tennis players: A quantitative psychological assessment," *The Sports Psychologist* 10 (4): 341-366.

INTRODUCTORY ACTIVITY

▶ Activity

Why Study Sport and Exercise Psychology?

Do this activity before reading chapter 1 of *Foundations of Sport and Exercise Psychology*.

Directions: Select one of the following scenarios for group discussion. In your group, derive a group response to the situation posed and summarize it in the space provided on the next page.

Scenario 1: Athletic Trainer—Mary Jo, the head athletic trainer at Campbell State College, has been working with Campbell's star running back, Kevin Jones, who is recovering from knee surgery. Kevin has made tremendous progress over the spring and summer and has achieved a 99% physical recovery. The coaches, however, have noticed that Kevin still favors his formerly injured knee in practice and is very hesitant when making cutbacks. Mary Jo knows that Kevin has physically recovered, but she's not sure how to help him regain his former confidence.

Scenario 2: Coach—Jeff is the point guard on the high school basketball team that you coach. For your team to repeat as league champions, Jeff needs to play well, especially in clutch situations. However, you have learned from coaching Jeff last season that he becomes very nervous in competition. In fact, the bigger the game or the more critical the situation, the more nervous Jeff becomes and the worse he plays. Your biggest coaching challenge this season will be helping Jeff learn to manage stress.

Scenario 3: Fitness Leader—Sally is serving in her second year as fitness director for the St. Peters Hospital Cardiac Rehabilitation Program. She spent countless hours in her first year organizing and initiating her aerobic fitness program for individuals recovering from cardiac arrest. The program was very well received by both the patients and hospital administration. Recently, however, Sally has become concerned about a very high lack of adherence on the part of her clients. They just don't seem to stick with their exercise programs after they start feeling better. As many as 60% are dropping out before they make exercise a lifelong habit. Sally must get her clients to adhere to their exercise regimes, but she doesn't know how. Problems like these were never discussed in her classes in exercise physiology or exercise program design for cardiac rehabilitation.

Scenario 4: Physical Educator—Bob has wanted to be a physical educator ever since he can remember. He is a student teacher this semester, and he is becoming increasingly frustrated. The high school students in his classes are totally out of shape and have no interest in learning lifelong sport skills and becoming physically fit. It is all Bob can do to get them to participate in the mild exercise program during their 40-minute classes held twice a week. Bob's goal for the semester is to get his sedentary students motivated to learn lifelong sport skills and engage in fitness activities.

Scenario 5: Sport Psychologist—Tom is a sport psychologist and long-time Chicago Cubs baseball fan. His dream consulting position has recently become available: The owners of the Cubs, frustrated by the lack of team cohesion, have asked Tom to submit a consulting proposal designed to improve team cohesion. Tom has a week to design a psychological skills training program to enhance team cohesion and, he hopes, secure his dream position as sport psychology consultant for the Chicago Cubs.

Proposed Solution for Handling Your Scenario:

INTRODUCTION

- Use this book as a road map to achieve two goals: (a) a better understanding of sport and exercise psychology and (b) knowledge of how to apply sport psychology in exercise settings.

- Remember that this study guide should be used to supplement your textbook. For more detailed discussions of the material covered here, refer to *Foundations of Sport and Exercise Psychology, Second Edition.*

- As you work through the exercises in this study guide, think about how the information fits into our model. Each piece is only part of the whole picture.

Activity 0.1

Assessing My Knowledge of Sport and Exercise Psychology

Do this activity before you begin to read the first chapter of *Foundations of Sport and Exercise Psychology.*

Directions: Use this short quiz to assess your current level of knowledge about sport and exercise psychology. Circle True (T) or False (F).

1. Sport and exercise psychology is a relatively new field, having its roots in the late 1970s.   T   F

2. Most teachers and coaches are very knowledgeable about how to implement psychological skills with students and athletes.   T   F

3. Regardless of the form of motivation, the more motivated an athlete or exerciser is the better.   T   F

4. We know little about the personality characteristics of great athletes.   T   F

5. Youth participation in sport has consistently been shown to facilitate the development of self-confidence and leadership.   T   F

6. When beginning a goal-setting program, a number of goals should be set to ensure success.   T   F

7. Imagery is the primary tool or technique used by today's sport psychology specialist.   T   F

8. Identifying and developing techniques for enhancing performance is the major focus of the sport psychology specialist.   T   F

9. To achieve peak performance, a team must be cohesive (i.e., tight-knit).   T   F

10. Running can be an effective method for managing clinical depression.   T   F

Answers to Selected Introduction Activities

Activity 0.1:   Assessing My Knowledge of Sport and Exercise Psychology

1. False. As we will soon learn, sport and exercise psychology has a long and rich history, dating back to the early part of this century.

2. False. In the past, teachers and coaches have had little sport and exercise psychology training. Thus, they simply told athletes to "relax" or "be confident," but seldom told them how to do so. Through courses using textbooks like this one, this state of affairs is starting to change.

3. False. While many forms of motivation lead to better performance, certain aspects of motivation are negatively related to performance and participation. Thus, being more motivated is not always better. We'll learn more about motivation when we discuss such topics as intrinsic motivation, achievement motivation, and arousal and stress.

4. True. While considerable research has been conducted in search of the ideal personality profile of the highly successful athletic competitor, few characteristics have been identified as common to all great athletes.

5. False. While participation in sport has the potential to facilitate the development of desirable psychological characteristics, such as self-confidence and leadership, it does not automatically do so and, in fact, may have negative effects. In this course, you'll learn how to structure the sport environment to enhance the personality development of the participant.

6. False. Although goal setting is a very effective technique for changing the behavior of sport and exercise participants, it is best to set only one or two goals when working with beginning goal-setters.

7. False. Imagery is a very important strategy used by today's sport psychologists, but it is only one of many strategies (e.g., goals, relaxation training) available to him or her.

8. False. As we will learn, the field of sport and exercise psychology has two general objectives. One is to understand how mental factors influence performance. A second is to understand how participation in sport and exercise influences psychological growth and development. For these reasons, it is inappropriate to think sport psychology involves only performance enhancement.

9. False. Cohesion can positively influence team performance, but performance has also been shown to increase cohesion. Some noncohesive teams have actually performed well.

10. True. Recent research shows that physical activity can be an effective treatment for clinical depression.

Getting Started

 **Chapter 1 Welcome to Sport and Exercise Psychology**

Welcome to Sport and Exercise Psychology

concepts

- Sport and exercise psychology is both the scientific study of the behavior of people engaged in sport and exercise activities and the application of the knowledge gained. It has two major objectives: (1) to understand how psychological factors affect a person's motor performance; and (2) to understand how participating in physical activity affects a person's psychological development.

- Clinical sport and exercise psychologists are specially trained to treat those athletes and exercisers who have severe emotional problems. Educational sport and exercise psychology specialists educate athletes and exercisers about psychological skills and their development.

- A theory is a set of interrelated facts presenting a systematic view of some phenomenon in order to describe, explain, and predict its future occurrences.

- Determining causal relationships is the main advantage provided by conducting scientific experiments over conducting studies.

- Several approaches can be taken to sport and exercise psychology, including social-psychological, psychophysiological, and cognitive-behavioral orientations.

- Professional practice knowledge is knowledge gained through experience and must be integrated with scientific knowledge to guide practice effectively.

- The science of teaching/coaching focuses on the use of general scientific principles.

- The art of teaching/coaching is recognizing when and how to individualize these general scientific principles.

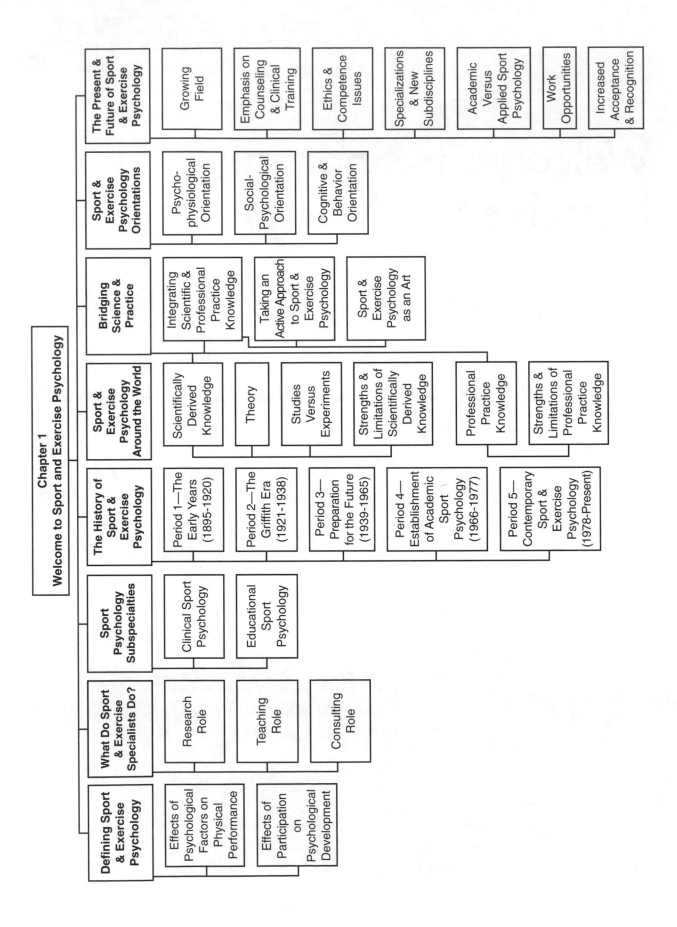

Chapter 1
Welcome to Sport and Exercise Psychology

Defining Sport & Exercise Psychology
- Effects of Psychological Factors on Physical Performance
- Effects of Participation on Psychological Development

What Do Sport & Exercise Specialists Do?
- Research Role
- Teaching Role
- Consulting Role

Sport Psychology Subspecialties
- Clinical Sport Psychology
- Educational Sport Psychology

The History of Sport & Exercise Psychology
- Period 1—The Early Years (1895-1920)
- Period 2—The Griffith Era (1921-1938)
- Period 3—Preparation for the Future (1939-1965)
- Period 4—Establishment of Academic Sport Psychology (1966-1977)
- Period 5—Contemporary Sport & Exercise Psychology (1978-Present)

Sport & Exercise Psychology Around the World
- Scientifically Derived Knowledge
- Theory
- Studies Versus Experiments
- Strengths & Limitations of Scientifically Derived Knowledge
- Professional Practice Knowledge
- Strengths & Limitations of Professional Practice Knowledge

Bridging Science & Practice
- Integrating Scientific & Professional Practice Knowledge
- Taking an Active Approach to Sport & Exercise Psychology
- Sport & Exercise Psychology as an Art

Sport & Exercise Psychology Orientations
- Psycho-physiological Orientation
- Social-Psychological Orientation
- Cognitive & Behavior Orientation

The Present & Future of Sport & Exercise Psychology
- Growing Field
- Emphasis on Counseling & Clinical Training
- Ethics & Competence Issues
- Specializations & New Subdisciplines
- Academic Versus Applied Sport Psychology
- Work Opportunities
- Increased Acceptance & Recognition

4

Activity 1.1

Understanding the Objectives of Sport and Exercise Psychology

Do this activity after reading chapter 1 of *Foundations of Sport and Exercise Psychology.*

Directions: Sport and exercise psychology is both the scientific study of the behavior of people engaged in sport and exercise activities and the application of the knowledge gained. Think of your own participation in competitive sport and physical activities (e.g., aerobics, fitness activities) and answer the following two questions about the major objectives of sport and exercise psychology.

1. How did psychological factors (e.g., confidence, anxiety, coaching comments) affect your performance in positive and negative ways?

2. How did your participation in the sport or physical activity affect your psychological development (e.g., self-confidence, leadership, personality)?

Charting the History of Sport and Exercise Psychology

Activity 1.2

Do this activity after reading pages 8 to 11 of *Foundations of Sport and Exercise Psychology.*

Directions: Referring to your book (see pages 8-11) draw a timeline that summarizes the five major periods in the history of sport and exercise psychology. Draw the timeline on a separate sheet of paper.

Library Research: Abstracting a Sport and Exercise Psychology Research Study

Activity 1.3

Do this activity after reading chapter 1 of *Foundations of Sport and Exercise Psychology.*

Directions: Go to the library and look for one of the sport and exercise psychology journals listed at the end of this activity. Select a research article (one that describes a study or experiment) that interests you and complete the following summary.

Title:

Author(s):

Journal:

Volume, pages:

Date of publication:

Summary of research study or experiment: (In your own words, describe what was done in the study or experiment—how the research was conducted.)

Summary of research findings:

Identify any implications for professional practice:

Journals that publish articles only on sport psychology: *Journal of Applied Sport Psychology*, *Journal of Sport and Exercise Psychology*, *The Sport Psychologist*, and *International Journal of Sport Psychology*.

Exercise and sport science journals that include articles from all exercise and sport science subdisciplines (such as biomechanics, exercise physiology, and sport sociology [Note: make sure you select a "psychological" article]): *Medicine and Science in Sport and Exercise*, and *Research Quarterly for Exercise and Sport*.

Designing a Sport Psychology Study and Experiment

Activity 1.4

Do this activity after reading pages 11 to 13 of *Foundations of Sport and Exercise Psychology*.

Directions: Reread the section entitled "Scientifically Derived Knowledge" (pages 11-12) and "Studies Versus Experiments" (pages 12-13) in *Foundations of Sport and Exercise Psychology*. Pick some question of interest that you have about sport and exercise psychology (e.g., How does imagery affect foul-shooting performance? How can you increase adherence to an exercise program? Does physical education teach children leadership skills?). Now design a study that examines that question by answering the questions listed below. Remember that a study involves an investigator observing or assessing factors or variables without changing the environment.

1. What is the sport psychological question you want to answer? (Be specific.)

2. What are the major factors or variables whose relationship you want to examine?

3. Whom will you study, or whom will the subjects be?

4. How will you collect the data?

5. Now, how could you change your study to make it an experiment? Remember, in an experiment the investigator manipulates the factors or variables along with observing them, then examines how changes in one variable affect changes in the others.

Welcome to Sport and Exercise Psychology Quiz

Do this activity after reading chapter 1 of *Foundations of Sport and Exercise Psychology.*

Directions: Read the descriptions, then select the lettered term that best matches each one. Use each term only once, although not all terms will be used.

a. reductionistic

b. internal validity

c. external validity

d. psychophysiological orientation

e. social-psychological orientation

f. cognitive-behavioral orientation

g. systematic observation

h. intuition

i. shared public experience

j. theory

____ 1. This orientation to sport and exercise psychology focuses on studying behavior by assuming that behavior is determined by both environment and thoughts, with thoughts and interpretation playing an especially important role.

____ 2. This term refers to the weakness of the scientific method in which a problem is reduced to smaller, manageable parts, which at times results in diminishing the whole picture.

____ 3. When a coach starts one player over another because it "feels" right.

____ 4. This characteristic of science focuses on the extent to which the results of an investigation can be attributed to the treatment utilized, usually judged by how well scientists conformed to the rules of science and how systematic and controlled they were in conducting their investigation.

____ 5. A set of interrelated facts presenting a systematic view of some phenomenon in order to describe, explain, and predict its future occurrences.

____ 6. Scientists focusing on this orientation to the field assume that behavior is determined by a complex interaction of the environment and one's personal makeup.

Learning About Sport and Exercise Psychology From Those Who've Been There

Activity 1.6

Do this activity after reading chapter 1 of *Foundations of Sport and Exercise Psychology.*

Directions: Professional practice knowledge in sport and exercise psychology is what one learns from working as a professional in sport and exercise science, whether that involves teaching, coaching, fitness leadership, or sports medicine. In this exercise you need to interview a sport and exercise science physical activity professional and ask the following questions. Summarize the responses in the space provided.

1. How prominently are mental factors involved in your work with the physical activity participants?

2. What psychological objectives do you have for those with whom you work (e.g., increase self-esteem)?

3. How do you motivate those with whom you work?

4. What are the major psychological problems you encounter in working with physical activity participants?

Comparing the Strengths and Limitations of Scientific and Professional Practice Knowledge

Activity 1.7

Do this activity after reading chapter 1 of *Foundations of Sport and Exercise Psychology.*

Directions: Form a group with two to three others from class and discuss the strengths and limitations of scientific and professional practice knowledge. Record your answers in the chart below.

Scientific Knowledge   **Professional Practice Knowledge**

Strengths: Strengths:

Limitations: Limitations:

Activity 1.8

Learn More About Sport and Exercise Psychology Organizations

Do this activity after reading chapter 1 of *Foundations of Sport and Exercise Psychology*.

Directions: Referring to the More Information box on page 18 of *Foundations of Sport and Exercise Psychology*, surf the Net and find one of the four sport psychology organizations listed at the top of the box. Answer the following questions.

1. Where is their next conference being held?

2. What publications do they offer, if any?

3. What other services/information do they contain on their Web site?

Activity 1.9

You Are the Expert: Predicting the Future

Do this activity after reading chapter 1 of *Foundations of Sport and Exercise Psychology*.

Directions: You are on a job interview and the potential employer indicates that her child (who is a senior in high school) is very interested in the field of sport psychology. From your résumé the employer sees that you have taken a course in the area. Answer the following questions that she asks of you.

1. What is sport and exercise psychology anyway?

2. What do sport and exercise psychologists do?

3. Who do sport and exercise psychologists work with?

4. Can any sport and exercise psychologist treat someone with an eating disorder?

5. What does the future of sport and exercise psychology have in store?

Answers to Selected Chapter 1 Activities

Activity 1.4:   Designing a Sport Psychology Study and Experiment

1. Is imagery associated with better foul-shooting performance in high school basketball players?

2. An imagery questionnaire that measures how much and how well athletes use imagery will be administered and foul-shooting percentages will be measured through an analysis of official scorebooks.

3. High school basketball players.

4. The imagery measure will be given at a practice prior to the season and performance (foul shots made) will be measured in every game. The relationship between a player's imagery scores (how often it is used and how well) and shooting percentage will be examined.

5. Use the same imagery and performance measures, but this time divide the players into equal groups and give one group (the imagery training group) a 2-week preseason imagery program plus normal basketball practice while the other group engages in normal practice. See if the imagery group has better imagery skills and better performance when compared to the no-imagery group.

Activity 1.5:   Welcome to Sport and Exercise Psychology Quiz

1. f
2. a
3. h
4. b
5. j
6. e

Activity 1.7:   Comparing the Strengths and Limitations of Scientific and Professional Practice Knowledge

Scientific Knowledge	Professional Practice Knowledge
Strengths:	*Strengths:*
Highly reliable	Holistic
Systematic and controlled	Innovative
Objective and unbiased	Immediate
Limitations:	*Limitations:*
Reductionistic	Less Reliable
Conservative, often slow to evolve	Lack of explanations
Lack of focus on external validity (practicality)	Greater susceptibility to bias

Activity 1.9: You Are the Expert: Predicting the Future

1. Sport and exercise psychology is both the scientific study of people and their behaviors in sport and exercise activities and the practical application of that knowledge. Sport and exercise psychologists seek to understand and help elite athletes, children, the physically and mentally disabled, seniors, and average participants achieve peak performance, personal satisfaction, and development through sport participation. (See text pages 4-5.)

2. Sport and exercise psychology specialists serve three primary roles in their professional activities: conducting research, teaching, and consulting. (See text pages 5-6.)

3. Sport and exercise psychologists work with elite athletes, children, the physically and mentally disabled, seniors, and average participants who want to achieve peak performance, personal satisfaction, and development through participation. (See text page 4.)

4. No, only clinical sport psychologists, who have specialized training to deal with people with severe emotional disorders. Educational sport psychologist are "mental coaches" who educate athletes and exercisers about psychological skills and their development. They are not trained to work with individuals who have severe emotional disorders. (See text pages 6-8.)

5. Although there are more full-time opportunities than ever before, only a limited number of full-time consulting positions are now available. Trends point to such future directions as an increased interest in psychological skills training for sport psychologists; increased emphasis on counseling and clinical training for sport psychologists; increased emphasis on ethics and competence; increased specialization; some continuing tension between academic and applied sport psychologists; and more qualitative research. (See text pages 16-19.)

Understanding Participants

Personality and Sport

concepts

- Personality is the sum or blend of those characteristics that make a person unique and is divided into three separate but related levels: (1) the psychological core; (2) typical responses; and (3) role-related behaviors.

- The "interactional" approach that views the situation and the individual's personality traits as joint codeterminants of behavior has been shown to be the most useful way to understand personality. Behavior is better predicted when we have knowledge of the specific situation and how the person responds to particular types of situations.

- Sport-specific measures of personality predict behavior in sport settings better than do general personality tests.

- Using personality inventories alone to select athletes for a team or to cut them from a team is an abuse of testing that should not be tolerated.

- Successful athletes, compared with their less successful counterparts, possess a variety of psychological skills and cognitive strategies, such as high self-confidence, better concentration and focus, and positive thoughts and imagery.

- To better understand one's personality, the sport and exercise science professional must consider personality traits and situations, be an informed consumer by understanding the strengths and limitations of personality testing, be a good communicator, be a good observer, and be knowledgeable about mental strategies.

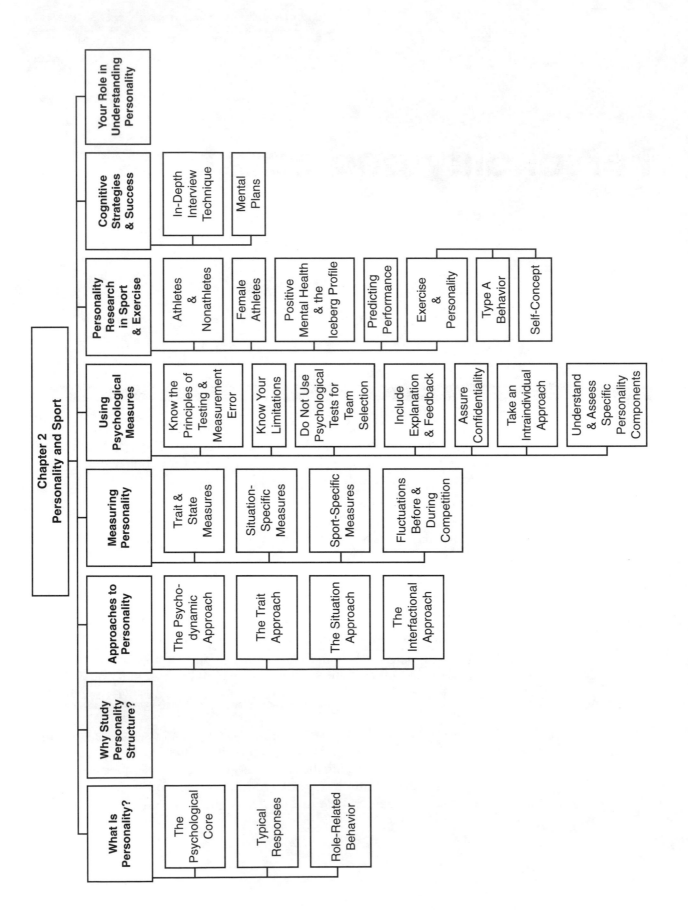

Chapter 2
Personality and Sport

What Is Personality?
- The Psychological Core
- Typical Responses
- Role-Related Behavior

Why Study Personality Structure?

Approaches to Personality
- The Psycho-dynamic Approach
- The Trait Approach
- The Situation Approach
- The Interfactional Approach

Measuring Personality
- Trait & State Measures
- Situation-Specific Measures
- Sport-Specific Measures
- Fluctuations Before & During Competition

Using Psychological Measures
- Know the Principles of Testing & Measurement Error
- Know Your Limitations
- Do Not Use Psychological Tests for Team Selection
- Include Explanation & Feedback
- Assure Confidentiality
- Take an Intraindividual Approach
- Understand & Assess Specific Personality Components

Personality Research in Sport & Exercise
- Athletes & Nonathletes
- Female Athletes
- Positive Mental Health & the Iceberg Profile
- Predicting Performance
- Exercise & Personality
- Type A Behavior
- Self-Concept

Cognitive Strategies & Success
- In-Depth Interview Technique
- Mental Plans

Your Role in Understanding Personality

The Structure of Personality: Taking a Look at Yourself

Activity 2.1

Do this activity before reading chapter 2 of *Foundations of Sport and Exercise Psychology*.

Directions: Do this exercise alone. Thinking of your own personality, identify characteristics that correspond to each of the following components of the structure of personality.

1. Role-related behaviors (How you act in different social situations—e.g., as coach or instructor, student, son or daughter, parent):

2. Typical responses (The way you typically respond in different situations):

3. Psychological core (Your most basic and deepest attitudes, values, interests, and motives):

Why Study Personality?

Activity 2.2

Do this activity after reading chapter 2 of *Foundations of Sport and Exercise Psychology*.

Directions: Working with a small group of classmates identify several reasons for why an understanding of participant or client personality would be useful to each of the following exercise and sport science professionals.

1. Athletic trainer/Physical therapist:

2. Fitness instructor:

3. Coach:

4. Physical educator:

5. Sport administrator:

Assessing Sport Confidence: How Confident Are You?

Activity 2.3

Do this activity after reading pages 30 to 34 of *Foundations of Sport and Exercise Psychology*.

Directions: Think about how self-confident you are when you compete in sport. Answer the questions below based on how confident you *generally feel* when you compete in your sport. Please try to determine how you *really* feel, not how you would like to feel. Compare your self-confidence level to the self-confidence level of *the most self-confident athlete you know*. Your answers will be kept confidential.

Scale: 1 = lowest; 5 = medium; 9 = highest (circle number from 1 to 9)

1. Compare your confidence in your ability to execute the skills necessary to be successful to the most confident athlete you know.

Low				*Medium*				*High*
1	2	3	4	5	6	7	8	9

2. Compare your confidence in your ability to make critical decisions during competition to the most confident athlete you know.

Low				*Medium*				*High*
1	2	3	4	5	6	7	8	9

3. Compare your confidence in your ability to perform under pressure to the most confident athlete you know.

Low				*Medium*				*High*
1	2	3	4	5	6	7	8	9

4. Compare your confidence in your ability to execute successful strategy to the most confident athlete you know.

Low				*Medium*				*High*
1	2	3	4	5	6	7	8	9

5. Compare your confidence in your ability to concentrate well enough to be successful to the most confident athlete you know.

Low				*Medium*				*High*
1	2	3	4	5	6	7	8	9

6. Compare your confidence in your ability to adapt to different game situations and still be successful to the most confident athlete you know.

Low				*Medium*				*High*
1	2	3	4	5	6	7	8	9

7. Compare your confidence in your ability to achieve your competitive goals to the most confident athlete you know.

Low				*Medium*				*High*
1	2	3	4	5	6	7	8	9

8. Compare your confidence in your ability to be successful to the most confident athlete you know.

Low				*Medium*				*High*
1	2	3	4	5	6	7	8	9

9. Compare your confidence in your ability to be consistently successful to the most confident athlete you know.

Low				*Medium*				*High*
1	2	3	4	5	6	7	8	9

10. Compare your confidence in your ability to think and respond successfully during competition to the most confident athlete you know.

Low				*Medium*				*High*
1	2	3	4	5	6	7	8	9

11. Compare your confidence in your ability to meet the challenge of competition to the most confident athlete you know.

Low				*Medium*				*High*
1	2	3	4	5	6	7	8	9

12. Compare your confidence in your ability to be successful even when the odds are against you to the most confident athlete you know.

Low				*Medium*				*High*
1	2	3	4	5	6	7	8	9

13. Compare your confidence in your ability to bounce back from performing poorly and be successful to the most confident athlete you know.

Low				*Medium*				*High*
1	2	3	4	5	6	7	8	9

Scoring: This is Vealey's Trait Sport-Confidence Inventory (TSCI), a measure of the degree of certainty individuals *usually* possess about their ability to succeed in sport. To see where you stand, simply add up the 13 numbers you circled to obtain a score ranging from a low of 13 to a high of 117.

_____ Your TSCI Score

Activity 2.4

Understanding the Iceberg Profile

Do this activity after reading page 38 of *Foundations of Sport and Exercise Psychology*.

Directions: Referring to the bottom half of figure 2.2 on page 39 of the *Foundations of Sport and Exercise Psychology* text, graph the profile of mood state results of more and less successful athletes in different colors on the figure below.

Looking at the graph, explain why this is referred to as the iceberg profile?

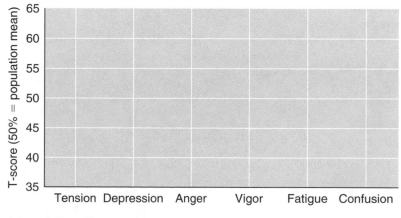

Adapted from Morgan, 1979.

Testing Your Understanding of Personality Research in Sport and Exercise

Activity 2.5

Do this activity after reading pages 37 to 43 of *Foundations of Sport and Exercise Psychology*.

Directions: After reading about sport personality research in the text, decide whether the following statements are True (T) or False (F).

1. No specific personality profile has been found that consistently distinguishes athletes from nonathletes.   T   F

2. Self-concept and trait anxiety differences have been shown to be evident between male and female athletes.   T   F

3. According to Morgan's mental health model, successful athletes exhibit greater positive mental health than less successful athletes.   T   F

4. An implication of Morgan's Profile of Mood States (POMS) research is that personality tests should be used to select athletes for teams.   T   F

5. The POMS instrument is not a useful means of monitoring the appropriateness of athlete training loads.   T   F

6. There is a link between Type B behavior and the incidence of cardiovascular disease.   T   F

7. Exercise and increased levels of fitness are associated with increases in self-esteem.   T   F

8. Olympic medalists differ from nonmedalists in that they internalize their stress-coping strategies to the extent that they become automatic.   T   F

Cognitive Strategies and Athletic Performance Interview

Activity 2.6

Do this activity after reading pages 41 to 43 of *Foundations of Sport and Exercise Psychology*.

Directions: Identify an athlete whom you can interview (the more elite the better), and ask him or her the following questions about cognitive strategies and athletic performance.

1. Think of a competition where you performed well. Indicate how you mentally prepared for the event. What did you specifically think or say to yourself to get mentally ready to compete?

2. Now think of a competition where you performed poorly. Indicate how you mentally prepared for the event. What did you specifically think or say to yourself to get ready to compete?

3. Did you feel stressed anytime before or during the competition? If so, how did you cope or deal with the stress of the competition? What strategies did you use?

Compare the results you found for questions 1, 2, and 3 with the application box on the bottom of page 43 of the text. How did your findings compare to the mental strategies of successful athletes summarized in the box?

Understanding the Personality of Others

Do this activity after reading chapter 2 of *Foundations of Sport and Exercise Psychology*.

Directions: The keys to understanding personality are communication and observation of behavior. Good communication and observation require a concerted effort, and this exercise is designed to help you become aware of this process. Working in pairs, think of your course instructor as you respond to the following:

1. Describe your instructor's personality characteristics.

2. Describe how you learned about his or her personality characteristics (e.g., through watching him or her teach, communicating during individual meetings, etc.).

3. Identify ways you could further validate your assessment of his or her personality or identify new aspects of it.

Answers to Selected Chapter 2 Activities

Activity 2.1: The Structure of Personality: Taking a Look at Yourself

1. Respectful (son or daughter); assertive (coach); outgoing (teacher)
2. Lighthearted; shy; even-tempered
3. Positive self-worth; belief in human rights; honesty

Activity 2.2:   Why Study Personality?

1. To better understand clients' adherence to rehabilitation and fears regarding re-injury.

2. To understand why some clients are very motivated and others are not. To help develop the self-esteem of a client with low self-esteem.

3. To select assistant coaches whose personalities are compatible with other coaching staff and team members. To make the most appropriate choice of a team captain.

4. To read students anxiety levels so that the appropriate amount of competition can be structured. To determine motives for student involvement.

5. To select a coach who best matches team-member personalities. To understand how to market to various individuals.

Activity 2.5:   Testing Your Understanding of Personality Research in Sport and Exercise

1. T; 2. F; 3. T; 4. F; 5. F; 6. F; 7. T; 8. T

Activity 2.7:   Understanding the Personality of Others

Since there are no standard answers to questions 1 and 2, answers are not provided.

3. *Identify ways you could further validate your assessment of his or her personality or identify new aspects of it.*

   - Interview my instructor

   - Ask other students who know him or her what they think his/her key personality characteristics are

   - Observe him or her in various settings (e.g., playing basketball, at a conference, in a committee meeting)

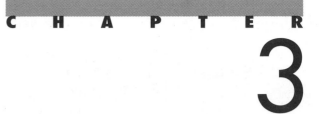

Motivation

concepts

- Motivation is the intensity and direction of effort.

- To enhance motivation you must analyze and respond not only to a participant's personality but also to the interaction of personal and situational characteristics.

- High-achievers select challenging tasks, prefer intermediate risks, and perform better when evaluated.

- An outcome goal orientation focuses on comparing performance with and defeating others, whereas a task goal orientation focuses on comparing performances with personal standards and personal task improvement. It is best to adopt a task orientation, which emphasizes comparisons with your own performance standards rather than with the performances of others.

- How performers explain or attribute their performance affects their expectations and emotional reactions, which in turn influences future achievement motivation.

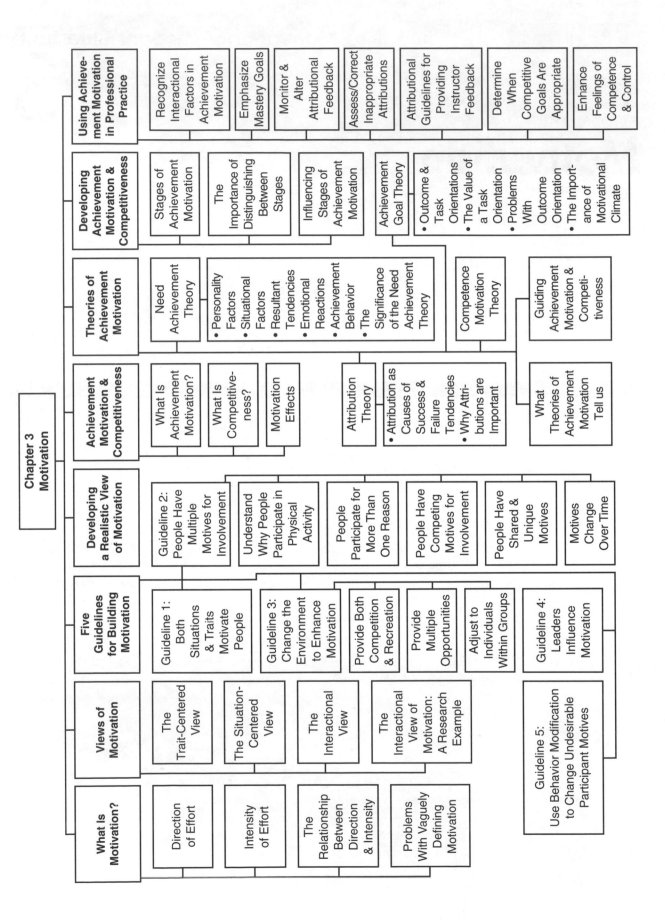

**Chapter 3
Motivation**

What Is Motivation?
- Direction of Effort
- Intensity of Effort
- The Relationship Between Direction & Intensity
- Problems With Vaguely Defining Motivation

Views of Motivation
- The Trait-Centered View
- The Situation-Centered View
- The Interactional View
- The Interactional View of Motivation: A Research Example

Five Guidelines for Building Motivation
- Guideline 1: Both Situations & Traits Motivate People
- Guideline 3: Change the Environment to Enhance Motivation
- Provide Both Competition & Recreation
- Provide Multiple Opportunities
- Adjust to Individuals Within Groups
- Guideline 4: Leaders Influence Motivation
- Guideline 5: Use Behavior Modification to Change Undesirable Participant Motives

Developing a Realistic View of Motivation
- Guideline 2: People Have Multiple Motives for Involvement
- Understand Why People Participate in Physical Activity
- People Participate for More Than One Reason
- People Have Competing Motives for Involvement
- People Have Shared & Unique Motives
- Motives Change Over Time

Achievement Motivation & Competitiveness
- What Is Achievement Motivation?
- What Is Competitiveness?
- Motivation Effects
- Attribution Theory
  - Attribution as Causes of Success & Failure
  - Tendencies
  - Why Attributions are Important
- What Theories of Achievement Motivation Tell us

Theories of Achievement Motivation
- Need Achievement Theory
  - Personality Factors
  - Situational Factors
  - Resultant Tendencies
  - Emotional Reactions
  - Achievement Behavior
  - The Significance of the Need Achievement Theory
- Competence Motivation Theory
- Guiding Achievement Motivation & Competitiveness

Developing Achievement Motivation & Competitiveness
- Stages of Achievement Motivation
- The Importance of Distinguishing Between Stages
- Influencing Stages of Achievement Motivation
- Achievement Goal Theory
  - Outcome & Task Orientations
  - The Value of a Task Orientation
  - Problems With Outcome Orientation
  - The Importance of Motivational Climate

Using Achievement Motivation in Professional Practice
- Recognize Interactional Factors in Achievement Motivation
- Emphasize Mastery Goals
- Monitor & Alter Attributional Feedback
- Assess/Correct Inappropriate Attributions
- Attributional Guidelines for Providing Instructor Feedback
- Determine When Competitive Goals Are Appropriate
- Enhance Feelings of Competence & Control

Food for Motivational Thought Questions

Do this activity after reading chapter 3 of *Foundations of Sport and Exercise Psychology.*

Directions: Answer the following questions based on your own experiences in sport and physical activity.

1. Give an example of how the *direction* of your effort has varied in various sport, physical education, or exercise settings.

2. Give an example of how the *intensity* of your effort has varied in various sport, physical education, or exercise settings.

3. What are the key points of the trait-centered view of motivation? Provide an example of what someone who holds that view might say.

4. What are the key points of the situation-centered view of motivation? Provide an example of what someone who holds that view might say.

5. What are the key points of the interactional view of motivation? Provide an example of what someone who holds that view might say.

Better Understanding Why People Participate in Sport and Exercise

Do this activity after reading pages 48 to 53 of *Foundations of Sport and Exercise Psychology.*

Directions: This exercise helps you identify various motives people have for participating in sport or exercise. Working in a small group, discuss the reasons that you and people you know participate in athletics or exercise. What situational or personal factors influence participation? What are the major motives for participation? What are some of the most unusual or unique motives?

Sport participation motives:

Exercise participation motives:

> Activity 3.3

Understanding Attributions

Do this activity after reading pages 59 to 60 of *Foundations of Sport and Exercise Psychology*.

Directions: Give an example of each of the following attribution categories.

1. Stability: Stable

2. Stability: Unstable

3. Locus of causality: Internal

4. Locus of causality: External

5. Locus of control: In one's control

6. Locus of control: Out of one's control

> Activity 3.4

Achievement Motivation and Competitiveness Terms and Theories Test

Do this activity after reading pages 57-65 of *Foundations of Sport and Exercise Psychology*.

Directions: Below is a list of terms and 10 fill-in-the blank questions. Write the name of the appropriate term in the fill-in-the blank answer space provided. Use each term only once, although not all terms will be used.

a. attributions

b. autonomous stage

c. outcome goal

d. integrated stage

e. task goal

f. need achievement

g. learned helplessness

h. social comparison

i. competence motivation theory

j. motivational climate

k. competitiveness attribution

l. stage theory

m. high achiever

n. goal orientation theory

o. low achiever

___ 1. This theory of achievement motivation focuses on the interaction of personal factors, such as the motive to achieve success/avoid failure, and situational factors, such as the probability and incentive value of success.

___ 2. How people explain their successes and failures.

___ 3. In this stage of achievement motivation the focus is on mastery of one's environment and self-testing.

___ 4. This type of goal emphasizes comparisons with others and defeating others.

___ 5. According to this theory of achievement motivation, it is best to adopt a task goal.

___ 6. This is an acquired condition in which a person perceives that his or her actions have no effect on the desired outcome or task.

___ 7. This type of goal emphasizes personal development and self-testing.

___ 8. This type of individual seeks challenging tasks and prefers intermediate risks.

___ 9. This view holds that people are motivated to feel worthy and that such feelings are the primary determinants of motivation.

___10. This includes such things as the tasks that learners are asked to perform, student-teacher authority patterns, recognition systems, student ability groupings, evaluation procedures, and time allotments for activities to be performed.

Case Study: Helping Dave Regain His Skiing Success

Activity 3.5

Do this activity after reading page 62 of *Foundations of Sport and Exercise Psychology*.

Directions: Read the case study on the bottom of page 62 of the text. Pretend that you are Dave's coach and devise a program for helping him regain his motivation by overcoming his outcome goal orientation. Record your response below.

Answers to Selected Chapter 3 Activities

Activity 3.1:   Food for Motivational Thought Questions

1. I did not go out for the track team because I did not like the new coach.

   Even though I don't like the water I went to swimming class because it was so hot out.

2. I tried my hardest for most of the game, but I gave up when we had no chance of winning.

   Even though I attended physical education class, I did not pay much attention or work very hard. But I was always totally focused for my aerobics class.

3. This view contends that motivated behavior is primarily a function of individual characteristics such as needs, goals, or personality characteristics. Someone holding this view might say that athletes are "real winners or losers," implying that they are or are not highly motivated.

4. This view holds that one's motivation is determined primarily by the situation. Someone holding it might say that he or she does not like physical education because the teacher is so negative or is always criticizing everyone.

5. The interactional view says that motivation results not solely from one's personality or the situation, but the interaction of these sets of factors. Someone holding this view might say that his or her team is not motivated as a result of a mismatch between the coaching tactics used and the motives of the individual players.

Activity 3.3: Understanding Attributions

1. I won because I am talented.
2. I won because I got a lucky break.
3. I learned the roundoff back handspring because of all my hard work.
4. I learned the roundoff back handspring because my teacher was so good.
5. I lost because I did not work hard enough.
6. I lost because I could not afford the equipment.

Activity 3.4: Achievement Motivation and Competitiveness Terms and Theories Test

1. f
2. a
3. b
4. c
5. n
6. g
7. e
8. m
9. i
10. j

4

Arousal, Stress, and Anxiety

concepts

- Trait anxiety is a behavioral disposition to view circumstances that are objectively not dangerous as threatening and then to respond with disproportionate state anxiety. Highly trait anxious people usually have more state anxiety in highly competitive, evaluative situations than do people with lower trait anxiety.

- State anxiety is moment-to-moment changes in feelings of nervousness, worry, and apprehension. It is associated with arousal of the body by cognitive state anxiety that focuses on worries and negative thoughts and somatic state anxiety that focuses on perceived physiological arousal.

- Stress occurs when there is a substantial imbalance between the physical demands placed on an individual and his or her response capability under conditions where failure to meet the demands has important consequences. The stress process is comprised of four interrelated stages: (1) environmental demand; (2) perception of demand; (3) stress response; and (4) behavioral consequences.

- Event importance and uncertainty are major situational stress sources (with more event importance and greater uncertainty associated with greater state anxiety). Trait anxiety, self-esteem, and social physique anxiety are major personal stress sources (with higher trait anxiety, lower self-esteem, and higher social physique anxiety associated with heightened state anxiety).

- The catastrophe model predicts that with low worry, increases in arousal or somatic state anxiety are related to performance in an inverted-U manner. With greater worry, the increases in arousal improve performance to an optimal threshold beyond which additional arousal causes a rapid and dramatic decline in performance—a catastrophe!

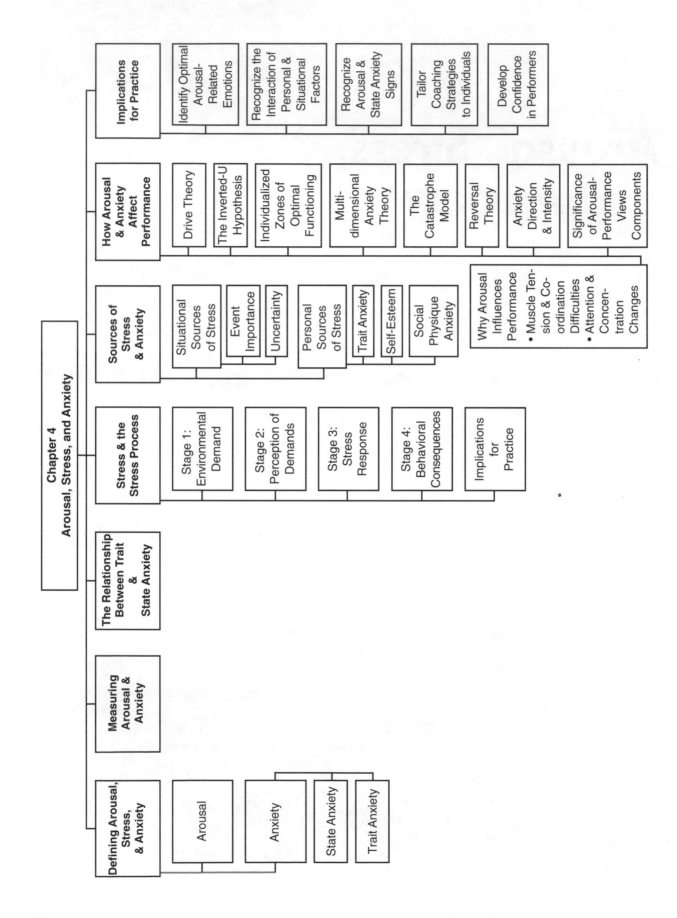

**Chapter 4
Arousal, Stress, and Anxiety**

Defining Arousal, Stress, & Anxiety

- Arousal
- Anxiety
  - State Anxiety
  - Trait Anxiety

Measuring Arousal & Anxiety

The Relationship Between Trait & State Anxiety

Stress & the Stress Process

- Stage 1: Environmental Demand
- Stage 2: Perception of Demands
- Stage 3: Stress Response
- Stage 4: Behavioral Consequences
- Implications for Practice

Sources of Stress & Anxiety

- Situational Sources of Stress
  - Event Importance
  - Uncertainty
- Personal Sources of Stress
  - Trait Anxiety
  - Self-Esteem
  - Social Physique Anxiety

How Arousal & Anxiety Affect Performance

- Drive Theory
- The Inverted-U Hypothesis
- Individualized Zones of Optimal Functioning
- Multi-dimensional Anxiety Theory
- The Catastrophe Model
- Reversal Theory
- Anxiety Direction & Intensity
- Significance of Arousal-Performance Views Components

- Why Arousal Influences Performance
  - Muscle Tension & Co-ordination Difficulties
  - Attention & Concen-tration Changes

Implications for Practice

- Identify Optimal Arousal-Related Emotions
- Recognize the Interaction of Personal & Situational Factors
- Recognize Arousal & State Anxiety Signs
- Tailor Coaching Strategies to Individuals
- Develop Confidence in Performers

- Arousal influences performance because heightened arousal is associated with increased muscle tension and coordination difficulties, narrowing of one's attention field, decreased environmental scanning, and a shift to the dominant attentional style, which may be inappropriate.

- Arousal management teaching and coaching strategies must be individualized. Sometimes arousal and state anxiety needs to be reduced, other times maintained, and still other times facilitated.

Assessing Your State: Taking a Look at Yourself

Activity 4.1

Do this activity after reading pages 72-74 of *Foundations of Sport and Exercise Psychology*.

Sport Competition Anxiety Test

Directions: Below are some statements about how people feel when they compete in sports and games. Read each statement and decide how often you feel this way when you compete in sports and games—*hardly ever, sometimes,* or *often*. If your choice is *hardly ever,* mark "A"; if your choice is *sometimes,* mark "B"; and if your choice is *often,* mark "C." There are no right or wrong answers. Do not spend too much time on any one statement.

	Hardly ever	**Sometimes**	**Often**
1. Competing against others is socially enjoyable.	A	B	C
2. Before I compete, I feel uneasy.	A	B	C
3. Before I compete I worry about not performing well.	A	B	C
4. I am a good sport person when I compete.	A	B	C
5. When I compete, I worry about making mistakes.	A	B	C
6. Before I compete I am calm.	A	B	C
7. Setting a goal is important when competing.	A	B	C
8. Before I compete I get a queasy feeling in my stomach.	A	B	C
9. Just before competing, I notice that my heart beats faster than usual.	A	B	C
10. I like to compete in games that demand considerable physical energy.	A	B	C
11. Before I compete I feel relaxed.	A	B	C
12. Before I compete I am nervous.	A	B	C
13. Team sports are more exciting than individual sports.	A	B	C
14. I get nervous wanting to start the game.	A	B	C
15. Before I compete I usually get uptight.	A	B	C

Scoring: This is the Sport Competition Anxiety Test (SCAT), a sport-specific measure of trait anxiety developed by Martens (1977). Items 1, 4, 7, 10, and 13 are filler items used to help disguise the purpose of the test. Cross these out, as they will not be used in the scoring. Items 2, 3, 5, 8, 9, 12, 14, and 15 are scored in the following manner: Hardly ever = 1 point; Sometimes = 2 points; Often = 3 points. For items 6 and 11, the scoring is reversed: (Often = 1 point; Sometimes = 2 points; Hardly ever = 3 points). Simply total the numbers for these 10 items to determine your trait anxiety score, which ranges from a low of 10 to a high of 30.

_____ = Your SCAT Score

Multidimensional Trait Anxiety (Sport Anxiety Scale)

Directions: A number of statements that athletes have used to describe their thoughts and feelings before or during competition are listed below. Read each statement and then circle the number to the right of the statement that indicates how you usually feel prior to or during competition. Some athletes feel they should not admit to feelings of nervousness or worry, but such reactions are actually quite common, even among professional athletes. To help us better understand reactions to competition, we ask you to share your true reactions with us. There are, therefore, no right or wrong answers. Do not spend too much time on any one statement.

	Not at all	Somewhat	Moderately so	Very Much so
1. I feel nervous.	1	2	3	4
2. I find myself thinking about unrelated thoughts.	1	2	3	4
3. I have self-doubts.	1	2	3	4
4. My body feels tense.	1	2	3	4
5. I am concerned that I may not do as well in competition as I could.	1	2	3	4
6. My mind wanders during sport competition.	1	2	3	4
7. While performing, I often do not pay attention to what's going on.	1	2	3	4
8. I feel tense in my stomach.	1	2	3	4
9. Thoughts of doing poorly interfere with my concentration during competition.	1	2	3	4
10. I am concerned about choking under pressure.	1	2	3	4
11. My heart races.	1	2	3	4
12. I feel my stomach sinking.	1	2	3	4
13. I'm concerned about performing poorly.	1	2	3	4
14. I have lapses in concentration because of nervousness.	1	2	3	4
15. I sometimes find myself trembling before or during a competitive event.	1	2	3	4
16. I'm worried about reaching my goal.	1	2	3	4
17. My body feels tight.	1	2	3	4
18. I'm concerned that others will be disappointed with my performances.	1	2	3	4
19. My stomach gets upset before or during competition.	1	2	3	4
20. I'm concerned I won't be able to concentrate.	1	2	3	4
21. My heart pounds before competition.	1	2	3	4

Scoring: This is the Sport Anxiety Scale, a multidimensional measure of trait anxiety developed by Smith, Smoll, and Schutz (1990). A cognitive, somatic, concentration disruption, and total score are calculated for this scale. Calculate and record your scores on each of the subscales listed below.

_____ Somatic trait anxiety: Sum items 1, 4, 8, 11, 12, 15, 17, 19, and 21.

_____ Worry trait anxiety: Sum items 3, 5, 9, 10, 13, 16, and 18.

_____ Concentration disruption trait anxiety: Sum items 2, 6, 7, 14, and 20.

_____ Total Trait Anxiety: Sum above three subscale scores.

The somatic trait anxiety subscale score ranges from a low of 9 to a high of 36. The worry trait anxiety subscale score ranges from a low of 7 to a high of 28. The concentration disruption trait anxiety subscale score ranges from a low of 5 to a high of 20. The total trait anxiety score ranges from a low of 21 to a high of 84.

State Anxiety Test

Directions: Complete the following scale on two separate occasions: a quiet time before practice when you are fairly relaxed, and a competitive situation you feel is highly stressful. If you are not currently active in competition, recall such situations as clearly as possible and record your responses.

Below are several statements that athletes use to describe their feelings before competition. Read each statement and circle the appropriate number to indicate how you feel right now, *at this moment*. There are no right or wrong answers. Do not spend too much time on any one statement.

	Not at all	Somewhat	Moderately so	Very Much so
1. I am concerned about this competition.	1	2	3	4
2. I feel nervous.	1	2	3	4
3. I feel at ease.	1	2	3	4
4. I have self-doubts.	1	2	3	4
5. I feel jittery.	1	2	3	4
6. I feel comfortable.	1	2	3	4
7. I am concerned I may not do as well in this competition as I could.	1	2	3	4
8. My body feels tense.	1	2	3	4
9. I feel self-confident.	1	2	3	4
10. I am concerned about losing.	1	2	3	4
11. I feel tense in my stomach.	1	2	3	4
12. I feel secure.	1	2	3	4
13. I am concerned about losing.	1	2	3	4
14. My body feels relaxed.	1	2	3	4
15. I'm confident I can meet the challenge.	1	2	3	4
16. I'm concerned about performing poorly.	1	2	3	4
17. My heart is racing.	1	2	3	4
18. I'm confident about performing well.	1	2	3	4
19. I'm worried about reaching my goal.	1	2	3	4
20. I feel my stomach sinking.	1	2	3	4
21. I feel mentally relaxed.	1	2	3	4
22. I'm concerned that others will be disappointed with my performance.	1	2	3	4
23. My hands are clammy.	1	2	3	4
24. I'm confident because I mentally picture myself reaching my goal.	1	2	3	4

25. I'm concerned I won't be able to concentrate.	1	2	3	4
26. My body feels tight.	1	2	3	4
27. I'm confident of coming through under pressure.	1	2	3	4

Scoring: The above scale is called the Competitive State Anxiety Inventory-2 (CSAI-2), a sports-specific state anxiety scale developed by Martens, Vealey, and Burton (1990). The scale divides anxiety into three components: cognitive anxiety, somatic anxiety, and a related component—self-confidence. Self-confidence tends to be the opposite of cognitive anxiety and is another important factor in managing stress. To score the CSAI-2, take all the scores for each item at face value *with the exception of item 14*, where you "reverse" the score. For example, if you circled 3, count that as 2 points (1 = 4, 2 = 3, 3 = 2, 4 = 1). Total your scores in the following manner:

___ Cognitive state anxiety: Sum items 1, 4, 7, 10, 13, 16, 19, 22, and 25.

___ Somatic state anxiety: Sum items 2, 5, 8, 11, 14, 17, 20, 23, 26.

___ Self-confidence anxiety: Sum items 3, 6 ,9, 12, 15, 18, 21, 24, and 27.

Your scores for each will range from 9 to 36, with 9 indicating low anxiety (confidence) and 36 indicating high anxiety confidence.

Activity 4.2 — Identifying Stress Sources

Do this activity after reading chapter 4 of *Foundations of Sport and Exercise Psychology*.

Directions: Teachers, exercise leaders, athletic trainers, and coaches often experience a lot of stress during their professional careers. One way to reduce the debilitating effects of stress is to identify the specific sources of stress and recognize when they begin. This exercise helps you identify sources of stress that you'll experience professionally. Working with three or four classmates, discuss and identify sources of stress that you think you may encounter in your professional life. Before beginning, identify what professional career your group will focus on (e.g., physical educator, coach, exercise instructor, athletic trainer, or sport psychology specialist).

1. What professional career will you focus on?

2. Identify five sources of stress you think those in this career typically encounter:

Activity 4.3 — Arousal, Stress, and Anxiety Matching Game

Do this activity after reading chapter 4 of *Foundations of Sport and Exercise Psychology*.

Directions: Write the name of the most appropriate term in the space provided. Use each term once.

a. arousal

b. stress

c. drive theory

d. reversal theory

e. low self-esteem

f. trait anxiety

g. cognitive state anxiety

h. somatic state anxiety

i. catastrophe model

j. zone of optimal functioning

k. inverted-U hypothesis

l. importance placed on performance

___ 1. An acquired behavioral disposition that predisposes an individual to view a wide range of objectively nondangerous circumstances as psychologically threatening and to respond to these with disproportionate state anxiety.

___ 2. A major *personal* source of stress.

___ 3. Performance is determined by the complex interaction of arousal and cognitive state anxiety; under conditions of high cognitive state anxiety or worry, a drastic drop in performance occurs as arousal increases beyond an optimal level.

___ 4. This view contends that the more aroused a performer is, the better he or she performs.

___ 5. A general physiological and psychological activation of the person that varies on a continuum from deep sleep to intense excitement.

___ 6. The degree to which one worries and has negative thoughts.

___ 7. The relationship between arousal and performance is dependent on the individual's interpretation of his or her arousal as positive or negative psychic energy.

___ 8. A major *situational* stress source.

___ 9. This view contends that the optimal level of state anxiety needed for best performance does not always occur at the midpoint of the state anxiety continuum.

___10. A substantial imbalance between the physical or psychological demands placed on an individual, and his or her response capability when failure to meet the demand has important consequences.

___11. This arousal-performance view contends that as arousal increases, performance increases up to a point of medium arousal level where best performance results, and that at high levels of arousal, performance declines.

___12. A moment-to-moment change in perceived physiological activation (not resulting from changes in physical activity level).

| **Activity 4.4** | **Signs and Symptoms of Increased Anxiety** |

Do this activity after reading pages 88 and 89 of *Foundations of Sport and Exercise Psychology.*

Directions: Forming a group with three or four classmates, ask each person in your group to complete the anxiety signs and symptoms checklist below by indicating which symptoms they experience during times of stress. Compare the symptoms and signs checked by each group member and note the ones most and least frequently cited.

Sign-Symptom	**Check if Applicable to You**	**# Of People in Group Listing**
Cold clammy hands	❑	_____
Constant need to urinate	❑	_____
Profuse sweating	❑	_____
Negative self-talk	❑	_____
Dazed look in eyes	❑	_____
Increased muscle tension	❑	_____
Inability to concentrate	❑	_____
Butterflies in stomach	❑	_____
Feel ill	❑	_____

Sign-Symptom	Check if Applicable to You	# Of People in Group Listing
Headache	❑	_____
Cotton mouth	❑	_____
Constantly sick	❑	_____
Sleeping difficulties	❑	_____
Consistently perform better in nonevaluative situations	❑	_____

Which symptoms and signs were the most and least frequently cited?

Answers to Selected Chapter 4 Activities

Activity 4.3:   Arousal, Stress, and Anxiety Matching Game

1. f
2. e
3. i
4. c
5. a
6. g
7. d
8. l
9. j
10. b
11. k
12. h

Understanding Sport and Exercise Environments

Competition and Cooperation

concepts

- Competition is "a social process that occurs when rewards are given to people on the basis of how their performances compare with the performances of others doing the same task or participating in the same event." Cooperation is "a social process through which performance is evaluated and rewarded in terms of the collective achievements of a group of people working together to reach a particular goal" (Coakley, 1994).

- Competition is a process comprised of four stages: (1) the objective competitive situation; (2) the subjective competitive situation; (3) the response; and (4) the consequences.

- Cooperative activities produce open communication, sharing, trust, friendship, and even enhanced performance more than competitive activities do. People will compete even when it is irrational to do so, and once competition breaks out it's hard to stop.

- Competition is inherently neither good nor bad. It is neither a productive nor a destructive strategy—it is simply a process. In youth sports especially, the quality of adult guidance is critical in determining whether competition positively or negatively affects the participants.

- Our social environment in large part influences competitive and cooperative behaviors. Children's competitive and cooperative behaviors are shaped by the reinforcement patterns of adults as well as by the particular cultural and social expectations placed on them.

- Cooperative games are viable alternatives that can provide complements to more traditional competitive games. Unorganized sport participation provides youngsters with opportunities for personal growth, decision-making, responsibility, and social interactions.

Chapter 5
Competition and Cooperation

Defining Competition & Cooperation

Competition Is a Process

- Stage 1: The Objective Competitive Situation
- Stage 2: The Subjective Competitive Situation
- Stage 3: Response
- Stage 4: Consequences
- Using Martens' Model

Psychological Studies of Competition & Cooperation

- Triplett's Cyclists
- Deutsch's Puzzles
- Competition & Aggression
- How Competition & Cooperation Score
- Experimental Games: Prisoner's Dilemma
- Overcoming the Dilemma
- Competitors Drawing in Cooperators
- Crosscultural Studies of Competition & Cooperation

Is Competition Good or Bad?

- Does Sport Competition Transfer to Life Skills and Achievement?
- Competition: Is It Different for Boys and Girls?
- Unstructured Sport: An Opportunity for Enhanced Cooperation & Growth

Enhancing Cooperation

- Component Structure of Games
  - Competitive Means—Competitive Ends
  - Cooperative Means—Competitive Ends
  - Individual Means—Competitive Ends
  - Individual Means—Individual Ends
  - Cooperative Means—Cooperative Ends
- Philosophy of Cooperative Games
- Cooperative Games: An Example
- Cooperative Games in the Gymnasium/Playing Field

What Is Competition?

Do this activity after reading page 96 of *Foundations of Sport and Exercise Psychology.*

Directions: Answer the following question about competition.

How would you define competition? (Give your own definition.)

Compare your definition to the reward and social evaluation definitions listed below and indicate with an "X" whether each of the following situations would qualify as competition according to each view.

Reward definition: A situation in which rewards are given to people based on their performance relative to other competitors.

Social evaluation definition: A situation in which a comparison of an individual's performance is made with some standard in the presence of at least one other person who can evaluate the comparison process.

Situation definition	Own	Reward	Social evaluation
Two university teams play football and the game does not end in a tie.	❑	❑	❑
Two university teams play basketball and the game ends.	❑	❑	❑
You are on a date playing tennis.	❑	❑	❑
You are alone playing golf.	❑	❑	❑
You are alone jogging.	❑	❑	❑
You are jogging with another without declaring a winner.	❑	❑	❑
Two university teams are playing for the NCAA championship.	❑	❑	❑
You and your roommate are playing tennis, with nothing at stake.	❑	❑	❑

Key Points About Defining Competition: Is Competition Good or Bad?—A Debate

Do this activity after reading chapter 5 of *Foundations of Sport and Exercise Psychology.*

Directions: Read the following statements:

Winning isn't everything. It's the only thing.

It doesn't matter whether you win or lose, it's how you play the game.

Win, win, win.

We tried our best.

Win at all costs.

Everybody should play.

As these statements show, there is no shortage of opinions about the roles that competition and cooperation should play in sport and in society as a whole. This exercise gives you a chance to debate these opinions. You have been divided into groups for the purpose of devising cogent, succinct arguments supporting the side to which you have been assigned. You will have about 10 to 15 minutes to talk within your groups. Then, group leaders from each side will face-off to debate in a point-counterpoint fashion. During the debate, record below the pros and cons of competition.

Pros

Cons

 **Activity 5.3**

Designing a Cooperative Game

Do this activity after reading chapter 5 of *Foundations of Sport and Exercise Psychology.*

Directions: Working with another classmate, restructure a traditional basketball game to make it less competitive and more cooperative. Use the five listed characteristics of cooperative games to help you.

1. Maximized participation

2. Maximized opportunities to learn the skills of the game

3. No emphasis on scoring

4. Maximized opportunities for success

5. Ample positive feedback

Answers to Selected Chapter 5 Activities

Activity 5.3:   Designing a Cooperative Game

1. You cannot score unless everyone on your team has touched the ball, or eight completed passes under defensive pressure counts as 2 points.

2. Each athlete serves as a guest coach one day and teaches his or her teammates or players to buddy up and provide feedback to one another.

3. Don't keep score, or switch members from one team to the next every 10 minutes.

4. Every player must play three different positions per game, or if everyone on the team scores the team gets 5 bonus points.

5. Players must reinforce one another at least five times per practice, or coach focuses on catching players doing things right.

Feedback, Reinforcement, and Intrinsic Motivation

concepts

- If doing something results in a good consequence such as being rewarded, people will tend to try to repeat the behavior to receive additional positive consequences. If doing something results in unpleasant consequences such as being punished, people will tend to try not to repeat the behavior so they can avoid more negative consequences.

- The principles of reinforcement are complex: people react differently to the same reinforcer; they may not be able to repeat a desired behavior; and they receive different reinforcers in different situations.

- In the early stages of learning, continuous and immediate reinforcement are desirable; in the later stages of learning, however, intermittent, immediate reinforcement is more effective.

- It is best to focus on a positive approach to influencing behavior. The potential drawbacks of punishment include arousing fear of failure, the punishers unknowingly acting as reinforcers by paying attention to undesirable behavior, and hindering the learning of skills.

- How recipients perceive rewards is critical in determining whether they will increase or decrease intrinsic motivation. Rewards that are perceived to control a person's behavior or suggest that the individual is not competent decrease intrinsic motivation, but rewards that emphasize the informational aspect and provide positive feedback about competence increase intrinsic motivation.

- Coaches, teachers, and exercise leaders can enhance intrinsic motivation by using verbal and nonverbal praise, involving participants in decision-making, setting realistic goals, making rewards contingent on performance, and varying the content and sequence of drills.

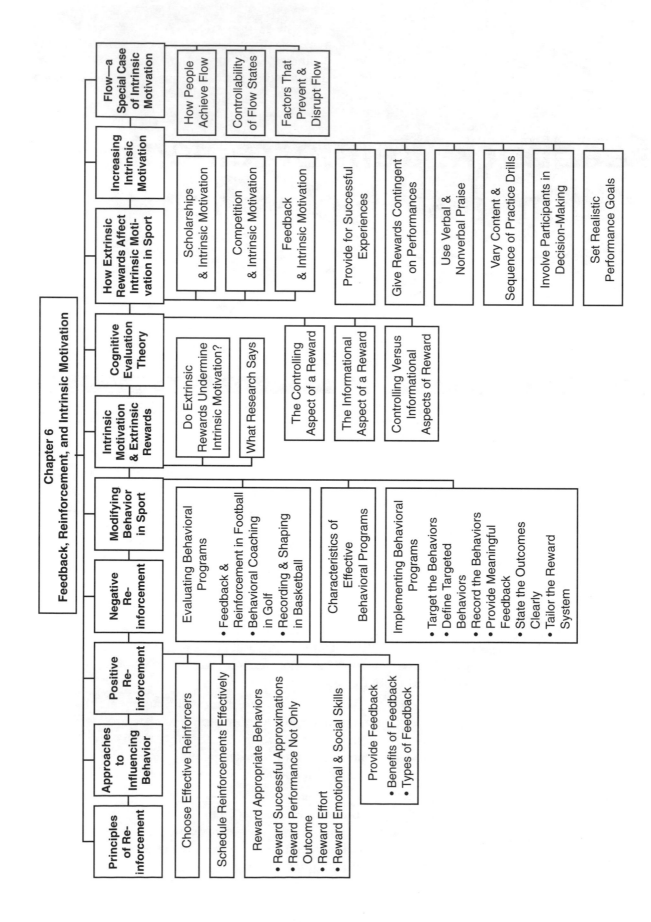

Chapter 6

Feedback, Reinforcement, and Intrinsic Motivation

- **Principles of Reinforcement**
- **Approaches to Influencing Behavior**
- **Positive Reinforcement**
  - Choose Effective Reinforcers
  - Schedule Reinforcements Effectively
  - Reward Appropriate Behaviors
    - Reward Successful Approximations
    - Reward Performance Not Only Outcome
    - Reward Effort
    - Reward Emotional & Social Skills
  - Provide Feedback
    - Benefits of Feedback
    - Types of Feedback
- **Negative Reinforcement**
- **Modifying Behavior in Sport**
  - Evaluating Behavioral Programs
    - Feedback & Reinforcement in Football
    - Behavioral Coaching in Golf
    - Recording & Shaping in Basketball
  - Characteristics of Effective Behavioral Programs
  - Implementing Behavioral Programs
    - Target the Behaviors
    - Define Targeted Behaviors
    - Record the Behaviors
    - Provide Meaningful Feedback
    - State the Outcomes Clearly
    - Tailor the Reward System
- **Intrinsic Motivation & Extrinsic Rewards**
  - Do Extrinsic Rewards Undermine Intrinsic Motivation?
  - What Research Says
- **Cognitive Evaluation Theory**
  - The Controlling Aspect of a Reward
  - The Informational Aspect of a Reward
  - Controlling Versus Informational Aspects of Reward
- **How Extrinsic Rewards Affect Intrinsic Motivation in Sport**
  - Scholarships & Intrinsic Motivation
  - Competition & Intrinsic Motivation
  - Feedback & Intrinsic Motivation
- **Increasing Intrinsic Motivation**
  - Provide for Successful Experiences
  - Give Rewards Contingent on Performances
  - Use Verbal & Nonverbal Praise
  - Vary Content & Sequence of Practice Drills
  - Involve Participants in Decision-Making
  - Set Realistic Performance Goals
- **Flow—a Special Case of Intrinsic Motivation**
  - How People Achieve Flow
  - Controllability of Flow States
  - Factors That Prevent & Disrupt Flow

- Flow epitomizes intrinsic motivation and occurs when a balance occurs between an individual's perceived capabilities and the challenge of the task. Confidence, optimal arousal, and focused attention help achieve flow states, and factors such as a self-critical attitude, distractions, and a lack of preparation prevent or disrupt flow.

Activity 6.1

What Types of Rewards Do You Prefer?

Do this activity after reading pages 115 to 121 of *Foundations of Sport and Exercise Psychology*.

Directions: Working alone, think of a sport or physical activity setting in which you are now participating or in the past have participated (this setting should involve structured coaching). Complete the Reward Preference Questionnaire listed on the following page.

Now analyze your responses and summarize what you have learned about your reinforcement preferences below.

Reward Preferences Questionnaire

Please answer these questions.

Social rewards

Place a check beside the kinds of approval that you like others to show.

_____ Facial signs (e.g., smiles, nods, winks)

_____ Hand and body signs (e.g., clapping hands, holding thumbs up, clasping hands overhead)

_____ Physical contact (e.g., a pat on the back, a handshake, a hug)

_____ Praise about yourself (e.g., you're smart, very helpful, a nice person)

_____ Praise about your athletic skills (e.g., you have a great throwing arm, backhand, jumpshot)

_____ Other (be specific) _____

Activity rewards

What activities would you like to do more often during practice? Explain why you would like to do them.

1. _____

2. _____

3. _____

4. _____

(Examples: Have free-swim time; shoot baskets for fun; help the coach set up equipment; help the coach score time trials; lead the group; demonstrate skills; change playing positions for fun)

Outings as rewards

Place a check beside the things you would like to do with the whole team.

_____ See a film about sports

_____ Tour a sports museum

_____ Have a local professional athlete visit with the team

_____ Go to a competition or sports event of professionals or high-ranking amateurs

_____ Visit a practice session for professional athletes

_____ Have a team party or dance

_____ Other events or activities (be specific) _____

_____

Material rewards

Place a check beside the things you would like to have or own.

_____ Team sweater

_____ Trophies

_____ Team uniform

_____ Personal chart that shows your progress from week to week

_____ Team jacket

_____ Other _____

Adapted from Martin and Lumsden, 1987.

| Activity 6.2 | # Understanding Punishment |

Do this activity before reading pages 121 to 123 of *Foundations of Sport and Exercise Psychology.*

Directions: During your professional career, you'll often encounter people engaging in undesirable or incorrect behavior. As a teacher, coach, or employer, you will be responsible for helping these people overcome such behavior. In this exercise, you'll practice applying principles of behavior modification, which will help you understand how punishment influences learning and performance. The exercise will also aid you in developing punishment guidelines that will help you identify effective methods of punishment. In groups, please discuss the questions listed below and come up with four to six guidelines for using punishment effectively.

1. Should we punish?

2. What behavior should be punished?

3. How should we punish?

4. What types of punishment should be used?

| Activity 6.3 | # Modifying Behavior in Sport and Exercise |

Do this activity before reading pages 124 to 128 of *Foundations of Sport and Exercise Psychology.*

Directions: Select a sport or physical activity skill that you wish to change (e.g., correct an inappropriate golf swing) and design a behavior modification program to change the behavior of interest. Address the issues listed below.

1. Specify the activity/target skill.

2. Define the specific target behaviors that you want to change.

3. Specify how you will record the behaviors.

4. Define what meaningful feedback will be provided.

5. State the outcomes of your program.

Activity 6.4

Testing Your Knowledge of Intrinsic Motivation

Do this activity after reading pages 128 to 134 of *Foundations of Sport and Exercise Psychology*.

Directions: Test your knowledge of intrinsic motivation by responding to the following questions.

1. Identify in what situations athletic scholarships increase intrinsic motivation.

2. Identify in what situations athletic scholarships decrease intrinsic motivation.

3. Explain how competitive success affects intrinsic motivation.

4. Explain how competitive failure affects intrinsic motivation.

5. Explain how feedback influences intrinsic motivation.

Activity 6.5

The Flow Experience

Do this activity after reading pages 134 to 139 of *Foundations of Sport and Exercise Psychology*.

Directions: Your instructor has asked some of your classmates to describe their sport experiences that involved the state of *flow*. As they discuss their experiences, place a mark in the space provided each time one of the following characteristics of flow is mentioned. Then determine the factors that seem to allow for or improve flow and those that seem to prevent it or interfere with it.

Flow Characteristics

_____ Complete absorption in the activity

_____ Merging of action and awareness

_____ Loss of self-consciousness

_____ A sense of control

_____ No goals or rewards external to the activity

_____ Effortless movement

Factors allowing for or improving flow:

Factors preventing or interfering with flow:

Answers to Selected Chapter 6 Activities

Activity 6.3: Modifying Behavior in Sport and Exercise

1. Appropriate jump shot form in basketball
2. a. Square up to the basket

   b. Release ball at peak height of jump

   c. Hand/wrist follow-through
3. Have a manager monitor practice and game shots taken, recording the frequency of target behaviors on all jump shots
4. a. Public recognition—Award players with best form by posting name on bulletin board

   b. Each week coach provides social reinforcement in practice for good form (e.g., "Good job")
5. Improved jump shooting

Activity 6.4: Testing Your Knowledge of Intrinsic Motivation

1. When the scholarship provides information about an athlete's competence, telling him or her that he or she is good. Also, when the scholarship is not used to leverage control over a player's behavior.
2. When the scholarship is used to control a player's behavior (e.g., win or lose your scholarship!). When they are not informational, or when they don't make a player feel special (e.g., because everybody gets one).
3. Competitive success tends to increase intrinsic motivation. However, wining is less important than how a person perceives how he or she played. If players perceive that they played well (regardless of wining or losing), intrinsic motivation increases.
4. Competitive failure tends to decrease intrinsic motivation. However, losing is less important than how a person perceives that he or she played—if players perceive that they played poorly (regardless of wining or losing), intrinsic motivation decreases.
5. Positive feedback increases intrinsic motivation.

Understanding Group Processes

7

Group and Team Dynamics

concepts

- The four stages that groups go through to move from a mere collection of individuals to a team include: forming, storming, norming, and performing. The distinguishing characteristics of sport and exercise groups are a collective identity, a sense of shared purpose or objectives, structured modes of communication, personal or task interdependence (or both), and interpersonal attraction.

- Two of the most important structural characteristics of groups are group roles (sets of behaviors required or expected of the person occupying a certain position in a group) and norms (levels of performance, or patterns of behaviors or beliefs held by the group). Effective teams have clearly defined roles and norms of high productivity.

- Team climate develops from how players perceive the interrelationships among the group members and is affected by social support, proximity, distinctiveness, fairness, and similarity.

- Social support functions to provide appraisal information, reassurance, and companionship; reduce uncertainty during times of stress; aid in mental and physical recovery; and improve communication skills.

- The abilities of individual team members are often not good predictors of how a team will perform. An individual's sense of contributing to the team effort can be maximized by using videotape, helping players understand their roles, and increasing identifiability.

- The Ringlemann effect is the phenomenon by which individual performance decreases as the number of people in the group increases.

- Social loafing occurs when a group puts forth less than 100% effort due to losses in motivation; there is a diffusion of responsibility and individuals feel that others within the group will pick up the slack.

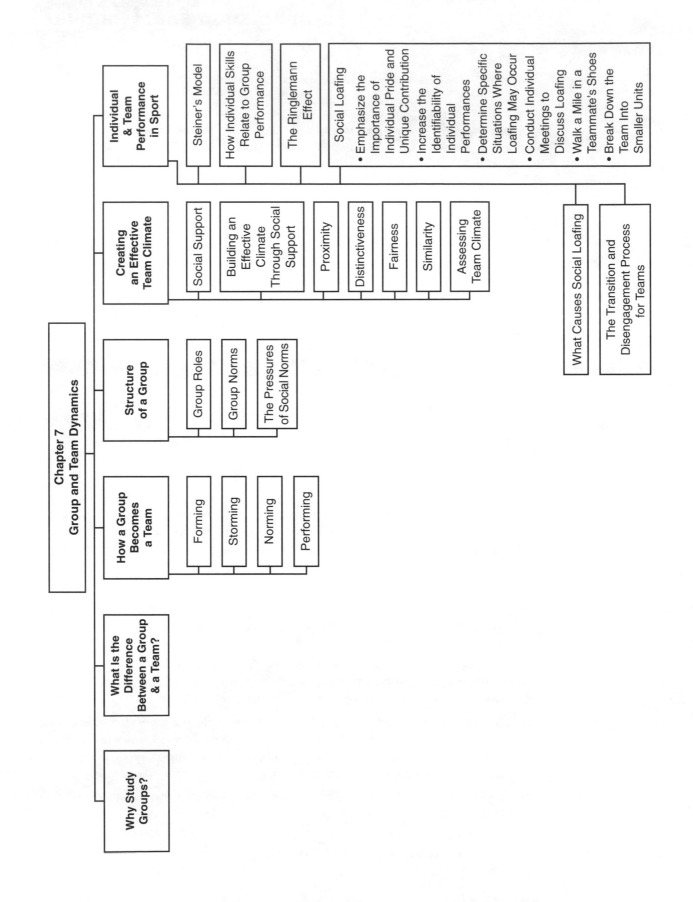

Chapter 7
Group and Team Dynamics

Why Study Groups?

What Is the Difference Between a Group & a Team?

How a Group Becomes a Team
- Forming
- Storming
- Norming
- Performing

Structure of a Group
- Group Roles
- Group Norms
- The Pressures of Social Norms

Creating an Effective Team Climate
- Social Support
- Building an Effective Climate Through Social Support
- Proximity
- Distinctiveness
- Fairness
- Similarity
- Assessing Team Climate

Individual & Team Performance in Sport
- Steiner's Model
- How Individual Skills Relate to Group Performance
- The Ringlemann Effect
- Social Loafing
  - Emphasize the Importance of Individual Pride and Unique Contribution
  - Increase the Identifiability of Individual Performances
  - Determine Specific Situations Where Loafing May Occur
  - Conduct Individual Meetings to Discuss Loafing
  - Walk a Mile in a Teammate's Shoes
  - Break Down the Team Into Smaller Units

What Causes Social Loafing

The Transition and Disengagement Process for Teams

Forming, Storming, Norming, and Performing

Do this activity after reading pages 145 to 148 of *Foundations of Sport and Exercise Psychology.*

Directions: Think of an athletic team or a group that you were a member of. Consider your experiences in this group and how the group developed over time. Indicate below what each of the stages of group formation (forming, storming, norming, and performing) was like for your team or group. (If your group skipped one or more of the stages, indicate this also.)

1. Forming

2. Storming

3. Norming

4. Performing

Developing Group Identity

Do this activity after reading pages 148 to 156 of *Foundations of Sport and Exercise Psychology.*

Directions: Working in groups, imagine that you have just become the coach of a basketball team, or that you are leading a group of clients in a cardiac rehabilitation program. You feel that things with the team or clients would go better if the group developed an identity. In the space below, describe specific ways you would go about helping a group form a sense of group identity.

Ways to enhance social support:

Ways to increase proximity:

Ways to increase group distinctiveness:

Ways to create a perception of fairness:

Ways to increase similarity:

Answers to Selected Chapter 7 Activities

Activity 7.2: Developing Group Identity

Ways to enhance social support:

1. Start a support group for patients (e.g., meet for lunch once a week). Invite patients at different phases of recovery to support one another.

2. Create a buddy system in which patients are paired up to exercise.

3. As a fitness leader, be sure to provide positive feedback to all clients and schedule time to listen to their concerns.

Ways to increase proximity:

Create a comfortable changing area (with nice chairs for lounging after exercise) where clients are likely to hang out and interact with one another.

Ways to increase group distinctiveness:

1. Provide program T-shirts

2. Have a group logo or slogan contest and print the best logo or slogan on T-shirts.

Ways to create a perception of fairness:

1. Be positive and upbeat and provid honest appraisals of current abilities.

2. Be sure to give all participants equal instructional time.

Ways to increase similarity:

Provide opportunities for clients who are well on the way to recovery to inform struggling clients about difficulties and roadblocks that they too faced. Also, have clients discuss their surgeries so that everyone involved sees that they are in the program for similar reasons.

Group Cohesion

concepts

- Cohesion is the total field of forces that acts on members to remain in the group. Task cohesion refers to the degree to which group members work together to achieve common goals and objectives, whereas social cohesion reflects the interpersonal attraction among group members.

- Various factors—environmental (team size, scholarships), personal (motivation, social background), team (team norms, team stability), and leadership (leadership style, leader's goals)—interact to affect the development of cohesion.

- The relationship between cohesion and performance is complex, but generally speaking, task cohesion is more closely related to performance than social cohesion, and cohesion is more important for interactive sports than coactive sports where it has little effect. The relationship between cohesion and performance also appears to be circular, with performance success leading to increased cohesion, which in turn leads to increased performance.

- Cohesion is positively related to a number of important factors, such as group-member satisfaction, conformity, social support, group goals, and stability. Teams higher in cohesion can better resist disruption than teams lower in cohesion, and teams that stay together tend to be more cohesive, which leads to improvements in performance.

- Exercise classes with high feelings of group cohesion have fewer dropouts and late arrivals than do classes low in cohesiveness.

- To build cohesion coaches and leaders should: communicate effectively; explain individual roles in team success; develop pride within subunits; set challenging group goals; encourage group identity; avoid formation of social cliques; avoid excessive turnover; conduct periodic team meetings; know team climate; and know something personal about each group member.

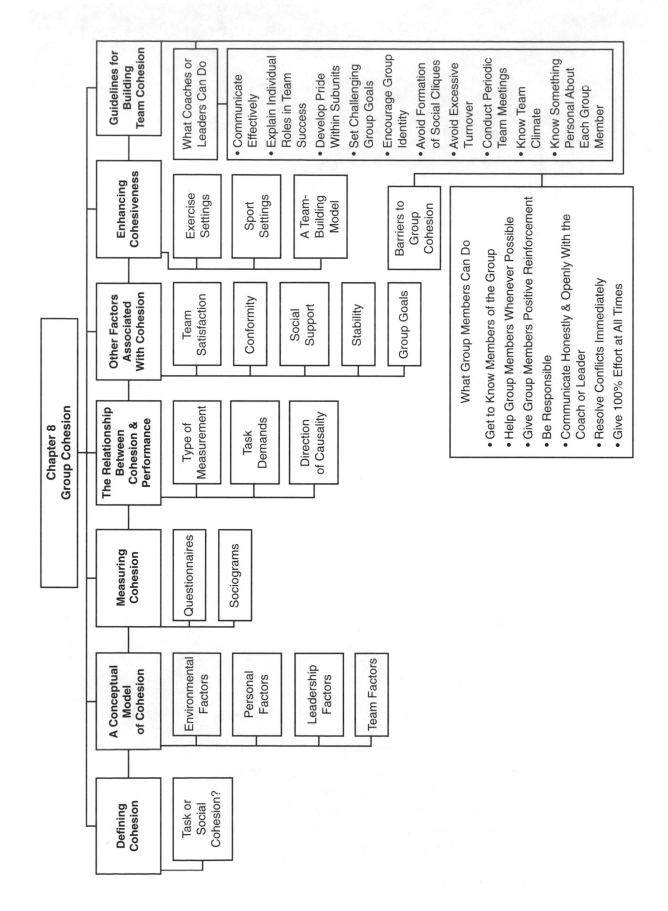

**Chapter 8
Group Cohesion**

Defining Cohesion

- Task or Social Cohesion?

A Conceptual Model of Cohesion

- Environmental Factors
- Personal Factors
- Leadership Factors
- Team Factors

Measuring Cohesion

- Questionnaires
- Sociograms

The Relationship Between Cohesion & Performance

- Type of Measurement
- Task Demands
- Direction of Causality

Other Factors Associated With Cohesion

- Team Satisfaction
- Conformity
- Social Support
- Stability
- Group Goals

Enhancing Cohesiveness

- Exercise Settings
- Sport Settings
- A Team-Building Model

Guidelines for Building Team Cohesion

- What Coaches or Leaders Can Do
  - Communicate Effectively
  - Explain Individual Roles in Team Success
  - Develop Pride Within Subunits
  - Set Challenging Group Goals
  - Encourage Group Identity
  - Avoid Formation of Social Cliques
  - Avoid Excessive Turnover
  - Conduct Periodic Team Meetings
  - Know Team Climate
  - Know Something Personal About Each Group Member

- Barriers to Group Cohesion

What Group Members Can Do

- Get to Know Members of the Group
- Help Group Members Whenever Possible
- Give Group Members Positive Reinforcement
- Be Responsible
- Communicate Honestly & Openly With the Coach or Leader
- Resolve Conflicts Immediately
- Give 100% Effort at All Times

Activity 8.1

Group Environment Questionnaire

Do this activity after reading chapter 8 of _Foundations of Sport and Exercise Psychology._

Directions: The Group Environment Questionnaire (GEQ) helps you assess your perceptions of an athletic team of which you are a member. If you are not currently participating on a team, answer the questions with respect to a team from your past. There are no right or wrong answers, so please give your immediate reaction. Some of the questions may seem repetitive, but please answer them all—and be as honest as possible.

The following questions help assess your feelings about your personal involvement with your team. Circle a number from 1 to 9 to indicate how much you agree with each statement. (Adapted from Carron, Brawley, and Widmeyer, 1985.)

Strongly agree   **Strongly disagree**

1. I do not enjoy being a part of the social activities of this team.

   1   2   3   4   5   6   7   8   9

2. I'm unhappy about the amount of playing time I get.

   1   2   3   4   5   6   7   8   9

3. I am not going to miss the members of this team when the season ends.

   1   2   3   4   5   6   7   8   9

4. I'm unhappy with my team's level of desire to win.

   1   2   3   4   5   6   7   8   9

5. Some of my best friends are on this team.

   1   2   3   4   5   6   7   8   9

6. This team does not give me enough opportunities to improve my personal performance.

   1   2   3   4   5   6   7   8   9

7. I enjoy other parties more than team parties.

   1   2   3   4   5   6   7   8   9

8. I like the style of play on this team.

   1   2   3   4   5   6   7   8   9

9. This team is one of my most important social groups.

   1   2   3   4   5   6   7   8   9

10. Our team is united in trying to reach its performance goals.

    1   2   3   4   5   6   7   8   9

11. Members of our team would rather go out on their own than get together as a team.

    1   2   3   4   5   6   7   8   9

12. We all take responsibility for any loss or poor performance by our team.

    1   2   3   4   5   6   7   8   9

13. Our team members rarely party together.

    1   2   3   4   5   6   7   8   9

14. Our team members have conflicting aspirations for the team's performance.

    1   2   3   4   5   6   7   8   9

15. Our team would like to spend time together in the off-season.

    1   2   3   4   5   6   7   8   9

16. If members of our team have problems in practice, everyone wants to help them so we can get back together again.

    1   2   3   4   5   6   7   8   9

17. Members of our team do not stick together outside of practices and games.

    1   2   3   4   5   6   7   8   9

18. Our team members do not communicate freely about each athlete's responsibilities during competition or practice.

    1   2   3   4   5   6   7   8   9

Scoring: The GEQ measures these four elements regarding how attractive a group is to its individual members: (1) *attraction to group—task*; (2) *attraction to group—social*; (3) *group integration—task*; and (4) *group integration—social*. To determine your score, simply add the numbers you circled for the questions in brackets below. However, items 1, 2, 3, 4, 6, 7, 8, 11, 13, 14, 17 and 18 should be reverse scored, which means that a 1 would equal 9 and a 9 would equal 1.

___ Individual Attraction to Group—Task [sum of scores for items 2 + 4 + 6 + 8; range = 4-36]

___ Individual Attraction to Group—Social [sum of scores for items 1 + 3 + 5 + 7 + 9; range = 5-45]

___ Group Integration—Task [sum of scores for items 10 + 12 + 14 + 16 + 18; range = 5-45]

___ Group Integration—Social [sum of scores for items 11 + 13 + 15 + 17; range = 4-36]

The higher your score on each subscale, the greater you reflect that dimension (e.g., a score of 31 on the Individual Attraction—Social scale means you are more socially attracted to the group than a score of 15 would indicate). Note that the Individual Attraction scales range from a low of 4 to a high of 36, whereas the Group Integration scales range from a low of 5 to a high of 45.

▶ Activity 8.2

Sociograms

Do this activity after reading pages 171 to 172 of *Foundations of Sport and Exercise Psychology.*

Directions: Mary, Beth, Athisa, Bethany, and Kim are all members of the same basketball team. You are interested in understanding their team cohesion and decide to use a sociogram to do so. Based on the responses outlined below, construct a sociogram like the one listed on page 172 of *Foundations of Sport and Exercise Psychology* (note, however, that you will not graph negative relationships). Those players chosen most frequently should be placed toward the center of the sociogram, and those chosen less frequently should be placed on the outside. Connect the players with arrows showing the direction of choice (an arrow pointing from Beth to Kim shows that Beth selected Kim, and an arrow pointing from Athisa to Beth shows that Athisa selected Beth. When two players select each other, arrows go in both directions.

The players are asked to name two people they would "most" like to room with on road trips.

Mary selects: Bethany and Kim

Beth selects: Bethany and Kim

Athisa selects: Mary and Kim

Bethany selects: Kim and Athisa

Kim selects: Athisa and Bethany

1. Diagram your sociogram here.

2. Who are the "most" popular players?

3. Who are the "least" popular players?

4. What implications would these facts have for a coach?

Activity 8.3

Building Team Cohesion

Do this activity after reading pages 179 to 185 of *Foundations of Sport and Exercise Psychology*.

Directions: Divide into groups. Working in your group, think of an exercise class (e.g., an aerobics class that meets three times a week) and imagine that you are the instructor. Identify ways to enhance cohesion in your class. Record your answers on a separate sheet of paper. Be specific.

Activity 8.4

Overcoming Barriers to Team Cohesion

Do this activity after reading chapter 8 of *Foundations of Sport and Exercise Psychology*.

Directions: Barriers to group cohesion are identified in the text. Working with a small group of classmates, derive strategies for overcoming these barriers.

1. A clash of personalities in the group:

2. A conflict of task or social roles among group members:

3. A breakdown in communication among group members or between the group leader and members:

4. One or more members struggling for power:

5. Frequent turnover of group members:

6. Disagreement on group goals and objectives:

Answers to Selected Chapter 8 Activities

Activity 8.2: Sociograms

1. Sociogram

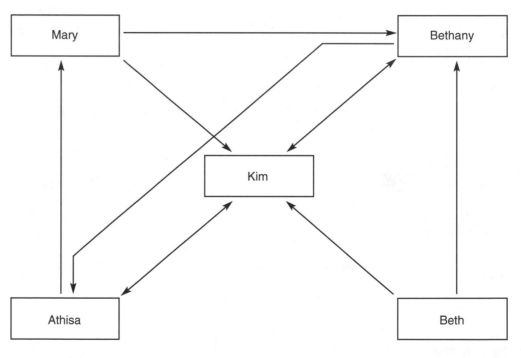

2. Kim and Bethany
3. Beth and Mary
4. No one seems to like Beth, and only one person seems to like Mary. The coach may want to determine why and implement some team-building strategies. Kim is the most popular player and might be a good person to talk with about what is going on with the team.

Activity 8.3: Building Team Cohesion

Ideas for enhancing cohesion through distinctiveness: (a) Create a group name for the class, like "Fitness Fanatics" or "Cardio Crew"; (b) Make up posters and slogans for the class, such as "lean, mean aerobic machines."

Ideas for enhancing cohesion through focusing on individual positions: (a) Divide the aerobics room up into areas for low-, medium-, and high-impact exercisers; (b) Have signs to label parts of the group so that newcomers can go to the area that they feel most comfortable in.

Ideas for enhancing cohesion through group norms: (a) Encourage class participants to become fitness friends and exercise outside of class; (b) Promote effort during class as a group characteristic (e.g., "This class is known for working hard. No slackers allowed!").

Ideas for enhancing cohesion through individual sacrifices: (a) Ask regular members to help newcomers become familiar with the step sequences; (b) Each class, ask one or two people from one of the subgroups (low-, medium-, high-impact exercisers) to set a goal for the day.

Ideas for enhancing cohesion through interaction and communication: (a) Have class members work in partners and have them introduce themselves; (b) Have regulars introduce new people to others in the group.

Activity 8.4: Overcoming Barriers to Team Cohesion

1. Refocus the group toward task goals—agree to disagree and put group goals ahead of personal differences.

   Have team members get to know one another on a personal level.

2. Clarify individual roles in relation to team success.

   Have athletes play in different positions so that they learn to appreciate the value of all positions.

3. Use Yukelson's (1997) DESC formula—have a team meeting to allow team members to describe the situation or problem, express feelings about the problem, specify desired changes, and discuss consequence.

   Have a "group disclosure" meeting to encourage athletes and leaders to share positive feelings towards other group members.

4. Avoid social cliques, which sometimes form when the team is losing, when athletes' needs are not being met, or when coaches treat certain athletes differently from others.

5. Make new team members feel welcome and part of the group.

   Encourage athletes to positively reinforce each other to create a supportive environment.

6. Involve team members in establishing goals.

   Have a team meeting to discuss disagreements; encourage athletes to be open and honest in their communication.

Leadership

concepts

- A leader is concerned with the direction of an organization, including its goals and objectives, and a manager takes care of such things as scheduling, budgeting, and organizing. Leaders affect participants by establishing interpersonal relationships, providing feedback, influencing the decision-making process, and providing motivation.

- Leaders have a variety of personality traits. Although there are not specific traits that make a leader successful, successful leaders tend to score high on both initiating structure and being considerate.

- A relationship-oriented leader focuses on developing and maintaining good interpersonal relationships; a task-oriented leader focuses on setting goals and getting the job done. The effectiveness of an individual's leadership style stems from its ability to match the needs of the situation.

- The Multidimensional Model of Sport Leadership holds that optimal performance and satisfaction are achieved when a leader's required, preferred, and actual behaviors are consistent with each other.

- Effective leadership in sport depends on the interactions of four sets of factors: the qualities of the leader, the leadership style, the situational factors, and the characteristics of the followers.

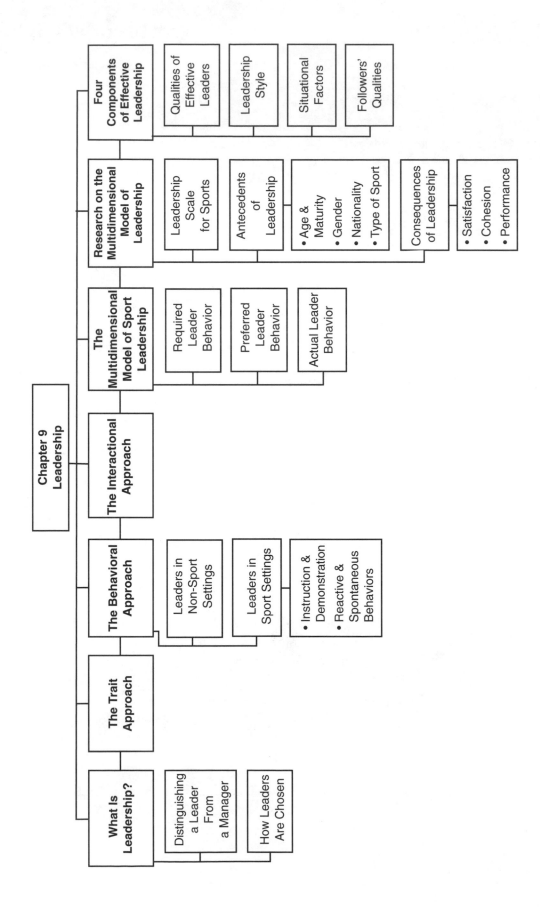

Chapter 9
Leadership

What Is Leadership?
- Distinguishing a Leader From a Manager
- How Leaders Are Chosen

The Trait Approach

The Behavioral Approach
- Leaders in Non-Sport Settings
- Leaders in Sport Settings
  - Instruction & Demonstration
  - Reactive & Spontaneous Behaviors

The Interactional Approach

The Multidimensional Model of Sport Leadership
- Required Leader Behavior
- Preferred Leader Behavior
- Actual Leader Behavior

Research on the Multidimensional Model of Leadership
- Leadership Scale for Sports
- Antecedents of Leadership
  - Age & Maturity
  - Gender
  - Nationality
  - Type of Sport
- Consequences of Leadership
  - Satisfaction
  - Cohesion
  - Performance

Four Components of Effective Leadership
- Qualities of Effective Leaders
- Leadership Style
- Situational Factors
- Followers' Qualities

Sport Leadership Quiz

Do this activity after reading chapter 9 of *Foundations of Sport and Exercise Psychology*.

Directions: Complete the following True/False quiz to test your knowledge of the antecedent and consequences found in the sport research on leadership. Circle True (T) or False (F).

1. As people get older and mature athletically, they increasingly prefer coaches who are more democratic and socially supportive.   T   F

2. Generous social support, rewarding of behavior, and democratic decision-making are generally associated with high satisfaction among athletes.   T   F

3. Losing teams need more social support from leaders.   T   F

4. Males prefer a democratic and participatory coaching style that allows them to help make decisions.   T   F

5. Athletes' preferences for social support decreases throughout high school and college.   T   F

6. Coaches perceived as high in training and instruction, democratic behavior, social support, and positive feedback, along with being low in autocratic behavior, had teams that were more cohesive.   T   F

7. Coaching effectiveness is rated highly by athletes when their coaches use the decision style preferred by the athletes.   T   F

8. No differences are evident among athletes from different cultures (e.g., American, Japanese, etc.) in terms of preferred leadership style.   T   F

9. Athletes who play coactive sports versus interactive sports prefer an autocratic coaching style.   T   F

10. Effective leadership style is influenced by a variety of personal and situational factors.   T   F

Assessing Your Leadership Characteristics

Do this activity after reading pages 194 to 200 of *Foundations of Sport and Exercise Psychology*.

Directions: In your text, Superbowl-winning football coach Bill Parcells' thoughts regarding the effective personality characteristics of great coaches are presented. Below, rate yourself on each of the characteristics he outlined with a rating of 1 (not at all like me), 2 (somewhat like me), or 3 (very much like me).

Rating	Leader's quality	Rating	Leader's quality
_____	Integrity	_____	Candor
_____	Flexibility	_____	Preparedness
_____	Loyalty	_____	Resourcefulness
_____	Confidence	_____	Self-discipline
_____	Accountability	_____	Patience

Relative to these characteristics, what are your strengths as a leader?

What are your potential weaknesses?

> **Activity 9.3**

Identifying Effective Leaders: Selecting a Team Captain

Do this activity after reading chapter 9 of *Foundations of Sport and Exercise Psychology*.

Directions: This exercise helps you learn how to identify effective leaders. Working in small groups, pick a sports team that all members in your group are familiar with (e.g., the university basketball team or a local professional team). Work together to identify any situational factors and member characteristics that might influence the leadership effectiveness of a captain on the team you picked. After doing this, identify the qualities you would want in a captain for this team and the style that he or she should use.

1. Describe the team your group will focus on:

2. What situational factors might influence a captain's leadership effectiveness?

3. What team member characteristics might influence leader effectiveness?

4. What characteristics would you want in a team captain for this team?

5. What leadership style would be most effective for this person to employ?

Answers to Selected Chapter 9 Activities

Activity 9.1:   Sport Leadership Quiz

1. False. (They prefer an autocratic style.)
2. True.
3. True (to sustain motivation).
4. False. (Females prefer this style.)
5. False. (It increases.)
6. True.
7. True.
8. False. (Differences are evident.)
9. False. (Athletes who play interactive sports prefer an autocratic style.)
10. True.

Communication

concepts

- People communicate in two ways: interpersonally and intrapersonally. Interpersonal communication involves both verbal and nonverbal communication, whereas intrapersonal communication is really communicating with oneself via self-talk.

- People send messages, both verbally and nonverbally. In nonverbal communication such factors as physical appearance, posture, gestures, body posturing, and touching are critical. Nonverbal messages are harder to hide and consciously control than verbal messages are, so they are often more accurate indicators of how a person feels. Effective verbal communication includes such characteristics as being clear and consistent, being direct, delivering messages immediately, and being consistent.

- Active listening is the most useful way to receive messages more effectively because the speaker feels that he or she is being heard, acknowledged, and provided with appropriate feedback. It involves attending to main and supporting ideas, acknowledging and responding, and giving appropriate feedback, as well as using nonverbal cues, such as eye contact and nodding your head to show understanding.

- Senders who convey messages that are ambiguous or inconsistent can cause communication breakdowns. Similarly, receivers who do not pay close attention to the message can also cause ineffective communication.

- Part of successfully resolving a problem is recognizing when and why a confrontation may be appropriate. The critical component is to express your feelings in a constructive manner by not getting angry, thinking before you speak, not attacking a person's character, being empathetic, proceeding gradually, and striving to understand the other person's position.

- Provide constructive criticism through a "sandwich approach," which consists of a positive statement, future-oriented instruction, and a compliment.

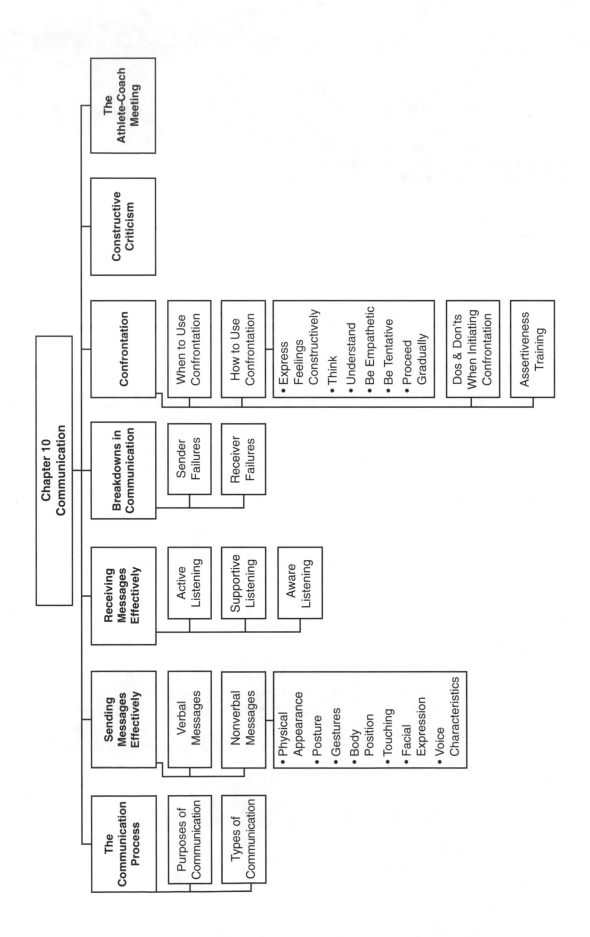

Chapter 10 Communication

The Communication Process
- Purposes of Communication
- Types of Communication

Sending Messages Effectively
- Verbal Messages
- Nonverbal Messages
  - Physical Appearance
  - Posture
  - Gestures
  - Body Position
  - Touching
  - Facial Expression
  - Voice Characteristics

Receiving Messages Effectively
- Active Listening
- Supportive Listening
- Aware Listening

Breakdowns in Communication
- Sender Failures
- Receiver Failures

Confrontation
- When to Use Confrontation
- How to Use Confrontation
  - Express Feelings Constructively
  - Think
  - Understand
  - Be Empathetic
  - Be Tentative
  - Proceed Gradually
- Dos & Don'ts When Initiating Confrontation
- Assertiveness Training

Constructive Criticism

The Athlete-Coach Meeting

Activity 10.1

Guidelines for Sending Verbal Messages

Do this activity after reading chapter 10 of *Foundations of Sport and Exercise Psychology.*

Directions: Think of two teachers or coaches you have had—one who you felt was a great communicator, and the other who you felt was an ineffective communicator. Compare the verbal communication skills of these two individuals by rating them both numerically (3 = Always, 2 = Sometimes, 1 = Never) in the spaces provided.

	Effective coach	Ineffective coach
1. Was direct	_____	_____
2. Owned the message (used I, my, etc.)	_____	_____
3. Was complete and specific	_____	_____
4. Was clear and consistent; avoided double messages	_____	_____
5. Stated his or her needs and feelings clearly	_____	_____
6. Separated fact from opinion	_____	_____
7. Focused on one thing at a time	_____	_____
8. Delivered messages immediately	_____	_____
9. Made sure messages did not contain hidden agendas	_____	_____
10. Was supportive	_____	_____
11. Was consistent with nonverbal messages	_____	_____
12. Reinforced message with repetition	_____	_____
13. Made message appropriate with your frame of reference	_____	_____
14. Looked for feedback that his or her message was accurately interpreted	_____	_____

What characteristics differed between the effective communicator and the ineffective communicator?

Activity 10.2

Assessing Your Listening Skills

Do this activity after reading chapter 10 of *Foundations of Sport and Exercise Psychology.*

Directions: Complete the listening skills test contained on the next page (this is the same one that is contained on page 211 of your text). When you complete and score the test, answer the following questions.

1. How well did you score on the test?

2. What specific items did you score well on (gave yourself "4" ratings)? That is, what are your listening strengths?

3. What specific items did you score poorly on (gave yourself "1" ratings)? That is, what are your listening weaknesses?

4. How could you improve the listening skill components you scored low on?

Listening Skills Test

Rating scale	Never	Seldom	Sometimes	Often
1. You find listening to others uninteresting.	1	2	3	4
2. You tend to focus attention on the speaker's delivery or appearance instead of the message.	1	2	3	4
3. You listen more for facts and details, often missing the main points that give the facts meaning.	1	2	3	4
4. You are easily distracted by other people talking, chewing gum, rattling paper, and so on.	1	2	3	4
5. You fake attention, looking at the speaker but thinking of other things.	1	2	3	4
6. You listen only to what is easy to understand.	1	2	3	4
7. Certain emotion-laden words interfere with your listening.	1	2	3	4
8. You hear a few sentences of another person's problems and immediately start thinking about all the advice you can give.	1	2	3	4
9. Your attention span is very short, so it is hard for you to listen for more than a few minutes.	1	2	3	4
10. You are quick to find things to disagree with, so you stop listening as you prepare your argument.	1	2	3	4
11. You try to placate the speaker by being supportive through head-nodding and uttering agreement, but you're really not involved.	1	2	3	4
12. You change the subject when you get bored or uncomfortable with it.	1	2	3	4
13. As soon as someone says anything that you think reflects negatively on you, you defend yourself.	1	2	3	4
14. You second-guess the speaker, trying to figure out what he or she *really* means.	1	2	3	4

Now add up your score. The following subjective scale will give you some help in determining how well you listen.

14–24	Excellent
25–34	Good
35–44	Fair
45–56	Weak

Reprinted from Martens, 1987.

Communication With Empathy and Understanding

Activity 10.3

Do this activity after reading chapter 10 of *Foundations of Sport and Exercise Psychology*.

Directions: In this exercise, you will practice the communication and confrontation skills you have discussed in class. Working in pairs, select three of the following situations and role-play the situation, one of you acting as the communicator and the other as the listener. The communicator should use such communication skills as empathy, "sandwiching," and active listening. Switch roles after each role-play.

Give each other feedback about how to effectively communicate and handle confrontations.

Situations:

1. Tell an athlete that she has been cut from the team.

2. Inform a client or patient that he is overweight and has several health risk factors.

3. Inform a PE student that he has poor hygiene and needs to shower.

4. Tell an injured athlete that her career is over.

5. Tell a teacher that he will be laid off in the upcoming year.

Check your partner's communication skills using these confrontation guidelines:

Dos and Don'ts When Initiating Confrontation

Dos

- Do convey that you value your relationship with the person.
- Do go slowly and think about what you want to communicate.
- Do try to understand the other person's position.
- Do listen carefully to what the other person is trying to communicate.

Don'ts

- Don't communicate the solution. Rather, focus on the problem. We are often overly anxious to tell others what they must do, instead of letting them figure it out.
- Don't stop communicating. Even if the confrontation isn't going as you planned, keep communicating about the problem in a constructive manner.
- Don't use "put-downs." Sarcasm and attacks usually alienate people. A confrontation is not a competition, and the idea is not to win it. The idea is to solve a problem together.
- Don't rely on nonverbal hints to communicate your thoughts. You need to be direct and forthright in communicating. Now is not the time for subtle nonverbal cues.

Adapted from Martens, 1987.

Activity 10.4

Constructive Criticism

Do this activity after reading pages 216 to 217 of *Foundations of Sport and Exercise Psychology*.

Directions: Provide an example of the three steps of the "sandwich approach" to constructive criticism to help the athlete discussed in the following scenario.

Jeff strikes out for the third time in a row. Frustrated, he did not keep his eye on the ball, repeatedly engaged in negative self-talk, and overstrided.

1. A positive statement:

2. Future-oriented instructions:

3. A compliment:

Answers to Selected Chapter 10 Activities

Activity 10.4:　Constructive Criticism

1　"It is tough striking out, but you hung in there and fouled off 2 or 3 pitches."

2. "Next time you're at bat I want you to focus on three things: (a) watch the ball from the moment the pitcher releases it; (b) take a shorter stride when you swing; and (c) regardless of the outcome of the swing, don't beat yourself up by saying or thinking anything negative to yourself."

3. "Hang in there—you're a battler and you'll get this."

Enhancing Performance

Introduction to Psychological Skills Training

concepts

- Psychological skills training refers to learning to systematically and consistently practice mental or psychological skills such as maintaining and focusing concentration, regulating arousal levels, enhancing confidence, and maintaining motivation. Psychological skills can be learned, but they must be practiced over time and integrated into a person's daily training regimen.

- A number of myths surround the development of psychological skills training (PST) and include: (a) PST is only for "problem" athletes; (b) PST is only for elite athletes; (c) PST provides "quick fix" solutions to complex problems; and (d) PST is only hocus-pocus and does not really work.

- The three general phases of PST include: (1) education (learning the importance of PST); (2) acquisition (learning mental skills); and (3) practice (using the mental skills during training—before using them in competition). The learning of psychological skills progresses from practices and simulations to actual competitions. Mental training should continue throughout an athlete's sport participation.

- There are a number of potential problems to be aware of when implementing PST programs. These include an athlete's lack of conviction, perceived lack of time to fit in the training program, lack of sport-specific knowledge (when a program is administered by a sport psychology consultant rather than a coach or athlete), and a lack of follow-up and evaluation.

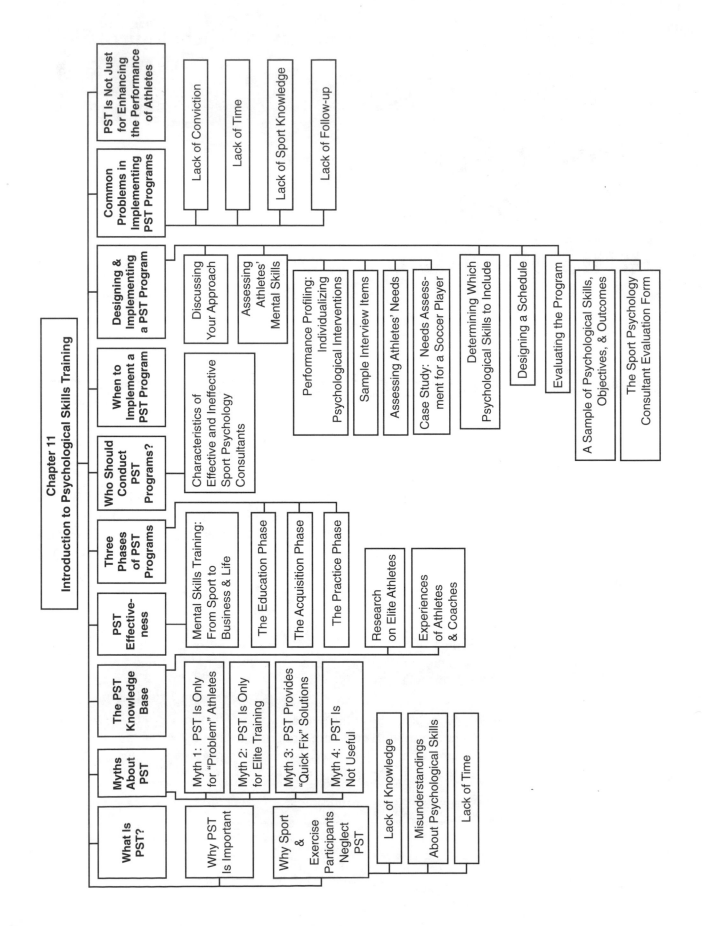

Chapter 11
Introduction to Psychological Skills Training

What Is PST?

Why PST Is Important

Why Sport & Exercise Participants Neglect PST

- Lack of Knowledge
- Misunderstandings About Psychological Skills
- Lack of Time

Myths About PST

- Myth 1: PST Is Only for "Problem" Athletes
- Myth 2: PST Is Only for Elite Training
- Myth 3: PST Provides "Quick Fix" Solutions
- Myth 4: PST Is Not Useful

The PST Knowledge Base

PST Effectiveness

- Mental Skills Training: From Sport to Business & Life
- The Education Phase
- The Acquisition Phase
- The Practice Phase

- Research on Elite Athletes
- Experiences of Athletes & Coaches

Three Phases of PST Programs

Who Should Conduct PST Programs?

- Characteristics of Effective and Ineffective Sport Psychology Consultants

When to Implement a PST Program

Designing & Implementing a PST Program

- Discussing Your Approach
- Assessing Athletes' Mental Skills

- Performance Profiling: Individualizing Psychological Interventions
- Sample Interview Items
- Assessing Athletes' Needs
- Case Study: Needs Assessment for a Soccer Player
- Determining Which Psychological Skills to Include
- Designing a Schedule
- Evaluating the Program

- A Sample of Psychological Skills, Objectives, & Outcomes
- The Sport Psychology Consultant Evaluation Form

Common Problems in Implementing PST Programs

- Lack of Conviction
- Lack of Time
- Lack of Sport Knowledge
- Lack of Follow-up

PST Is Not Just for Enhancing the Performance of Athletes

| Activity 11.1 | **Assessing Your Sport Psychological Skills** |

Do this activity after reading chapter 11 of *Foundations of Sport and Exercise Psychology.*

Directions: A number of statements that athletes have used to describe their experiences are given below. Please read each statement carefully, and then recall as accurately as possible how often you experience the same thing. There are no right or wrong answers. Do not spend too much time on any one statement.

Please circle how often you have these experiences when playing sports.

1. On a daily or weekly basis, I set very specific goals for myself that guide what I do.

   Almost never　　　　Sometimes　　　　Often　　　　Almost always

2. I get the most out of my talent and skill.

   Almost never　　　　Sometimes　　　　Often　　　　Almost always

3. When a coach or manager tells me how to correct a mistake I've made, I tend to take it personally and feel upset.

   Almost never　　　　Sometimes　　　　Often　　　　Almost always

4. When I'm playing sports, I can focus my attention and block out distractions.

   Almost never　　　　Sometimes　　　　Often　　　　Almost always

5. I remain positive and enthusiastic during competition, no matter how badly things are going.

   Almost never　　　　Sometimes　　　　Often　　　　Almost always

6. I tend to play better under pressure because I think more clearly.

   Almost never　　　　Sometimes　　　　Often　　　　Almost always

7. I worry quite a bit about what others think of my performance.

   Almost never　　　　Sometimes　　　　Often　　　　Almost always

8. I tend to do lots of planning about how to reach my goals.

   Almost never　　　　Sometimes　　　　Often　　　　Almost always

9. I feel confident that I will play well.

   Almost never　　　　Sometimes　　　　Often　　　　Almost always

10. When a coach or manager criticizes me, I become upset rather than feel helped.

    Almost never　　　　Sometimes　　　　Often　　　　Almost always

11. It is easy for me to keep distracting thoughts from interfering with something I am watching or listening to.

    Almost never　　　　Sometimes　　　　Often　　　　Almost always

12. I put a lot of pressure on myself by worrying about how I will perform.

    Almost never　　　　Sometimes　　　　Often　　　　Almost always

13. I set my own performance goals for each practice.

    Almost never　　　　Sometimes　　　　Often　　　　Almost always

14. I don't have to be pushed to practice or play hard; I give 100%.

    Almost never　　　　Sometimes　　　　Often　　　　Almost always

15. If a coach criticizes or yells at me, I correct the mistake without getting upset about it.

    Almost never　　　　Sometimes　　　　Often　　　　Almost always

16. I handle unexpected situations in my sport very well.

    Almost never　　　　Sometimes　　　　Often　　　　Almost always

17. When things are going badly, I tell myself to keep calm, and this works for me.

    Almost never   Sometimes   Often   Almost always

18. The more pressure there is during a game, the more I enjoy it.

    Almost never   Sometimes   Often   Almost always

19. While competing, I worry about making mistakes or failing to come through.

    Almost never   Sometimes   Often   Almost always

20. I have my own game plan worked out in my head long before the game begins.

    Almost never   Sometimes   Often   Almost always

21. When I feel myself getting too tense, I can quickly relax my body and calm myself.

    Almost never   Sometimes   Often   Almost always

22. To me, pressure situations are challenges that I welcome.

    Almost never   Sometimes   Often   Almost always

23. I think about and imagine what will happen if I fail or screw up.

    Almost never   Sometimes   Often   Almost always

24. I maintain emotional control regardless of how things are going for me.

    Almost never   Sometimes   Often   Almost always

25. It is easy for me to direct my attention and focus on a single object or person.

    Almost never   Sometimes   Often   Almost always

26. When I fail to reach my goals, it makes me try even harder.

    Almost never   Sometimes   Often   Almost always

27. I improve my skills by listening carefully to advice and instruction from coaches and managers.

    Almost never   Sometimes   Often   Almost always

28. I make fewer mistakes when the pressure is on because I concentrate better.

    Almost never   Sometimes   Often   Almost always

Scoring: This is the Athletic Coping Skills Inventory (ACSI), a measure of an athlete's psychological skills, developed by Smith et al. (1994). Determine your score on the following subscales by adding the scores on the question numbers identified. Also, note the following numerical scales associated with your ratings.

0 = Almost never

1 = Sometimes

2 = Often

3 = Almost always

Finally, note that an * after a question number signifies a reversed scored item (that is, 0 = Almost *always*, 3 = almost *never*, and so on).

_____ Coping With Adversity: This subscale assesses if an athlete remains positive and enthusiastic even when things are going badly, remains calm and controlled, and can quickly bounce back from mistakes and setbacks.

(Sum Scores on questions 5, 17, 21, and 24, and place the total in the blank provided.)

_____ Coachability: Assesses if an athlete is open to and learns from instruction, and accepts constructive criticism without taking it personally and becoming upset.

(Sum scores on questions 3*, 10*, 15, and 27, and place the total in the blank provided.)

_____ Concentration: This subscale reflects whether an athlete becomes easily distracted, and is able to focus on the task at hand in both practice and game situations, even when adverse or unexpected situations occur.

(Sum scores on questions 4, 11, 16, and 25, and place the total in the blank provided.)

_____ Confidence and Achievement Motivation: Measures if an athlete is confident and positively motivated, consistently gives 100% during practices and games, and works hard to improve his or her skills.

(Sum scores on questions 2, 9, 14, and 26, and place the total in the blank provided.)

_____ Goal Setting and Mental Preparation: Assesses whether an athlete sets and works toward specific performance goals, plans and mentally prepares for games, and clearly has a "game plan" for performing well.

(Sum scores on questions 1, 8, 13, and 20, and place the total in the blank provided.)

_____ Peaking Under Pressure: Measures if an athlete is challenged rather than threatened by pressure situations and performs well under pressure—a clutch performer.

(Sum scores on questions 6, 18, 22, and 28, and place the total in the blank provided.)

_____ Freedom From Worry: Assesses whether an athlete puts pressure on him or herself by worrying about performing poorly or making mistakes; worries about what others will think if he or she performs poorly.

(Sum scores on questions 7*, 12*, 19*, and 23*, and place the total in the blank provided.)

_____ Total score or sum of subscales

Scores range from a low of 0 to a high of 12 on each subscale, with higher scores indicating greater strengths on that subscale. The score for the total scale ranges from a low of 0 to a high of 84, with higher scores signifying greater strength.

Activity 11.2

Solving Common Problems in Psychological Skills Training

Do this activity after reading chapter 11 of _Foundations of Sport and Exercise Psychology._

Directions: You are implementing a Psychological Skills Training Program for a high school soccer team. Discuss how you could overcome each of the following psychological skills training problems.

1. Lack of conviction:

2. Lack of time:

3. Lack of sport knowledge:

4. Lack of follow-up:

Expanding Psychological Skills Training Beyond Sport

Activity 11.3

Do this activity after reading chapter 11 of *Foundations of Sport and Exercise Psychology.*

Directions: Form a small group with three to four classmates. In your group, select one of the following non-sport psychological skills training situations and design a PST program for that situation. Record your program design in the space provided. Be specific in outlining how you would set up, implement, and evaluate the program's success.

1. A physical educator wishes to use relaxation training with a hyperactive sixth-grade student.

2. A physical therapist/athletic trainer wants to build confidence in an athlete who is rehabilitating from a knee injury.

3. A fitness instructor wants to improve the level of motivation of one of her sedentary clients.

Answers to Selected Chapter 11 Activities

Activity 11.2: Solving Common Problems in Psychological Skills Training

1. I would point out that the U.S. women's soccer team that won the Gold Medal in 1996 in Atlanta used a Psychological Skills Training program. I would also point out that the entire world saw Mark McGuire use imagery prior to breaking the home run record in major league baseball.

2. I would carry out some of the mental skills training work during regular practice time to demonstrate the coaches commitment to developing mental skills. I would meet with each player to determine specific times during the week that they could devote to mental skills training.

3. I would do an Internet search to find soccer-specific mental skills training articles. I would highlight quotes from players and coaches on mental skills and lessons that were contained in soccer magazine by posting them in the locker room.

4. I would schedule weekly mental skills training meetings.

Activity 11.3: Expanding Psychological Skills Training Beyond Sport

2. *A fitness instructor wants to improve the level of motivation of one of her sedentary clients.*

Begin by assessing the client's needs, interests, and knowledge base. Through observation and interview, find out what motivates the client, why she is there, what she wants to achieve, what her expectations are, and what her knowledge of exercise is. Based on this information, assist the client in long- and short-term goal-setting. When setting goals be sure to explore the factors that might assist and detract from her efforts. Using her long-term goal, create a client contract that allows her to invest herself in achieving the goal. Have the client set aside the first five minutes of each workout to review her long-term goal. At the end of each workout session have her briefly review her goal compliance and achievement. Set up a regular schedule to meet, evaluate, and possibly reassess the goals and the goal plan.

Arousal Regulation

concepts

- A number of techniques have been developed to reduce anxiety and can easily be used in sport and exercise settings. The ones most often used to cope with somatic anxiety are progressive relaxation, breath control, and biofeedback. The most prevalent cognitive anxiety-reduction techniques include the relaxation response and autogenic training. Two multimodal anxiety management packages that use a variety of techniques are (1) cognitive-affective stress management and (2) stress-inoculation training.

- To effectively cope with unforeseen events, individuals need an array of coping strategies. Two major coping categories are problem- and emotion-focused coping. Problem-focused coping involves efforts to alter or mange the problem that is causing stress, such as goal-setting or time management. Emotion-focused coping involves regulating the emotional responses to the problem causing the stress.

- The matching hypothesis states that anxiety-management techniques should be matched to the particular anxiety type experienced—that is, somatic or cognitive anxiety. Specifically, cognitive anxiety should be treated with mental relaxation and somatic anxiety with physical relaxation techniques.

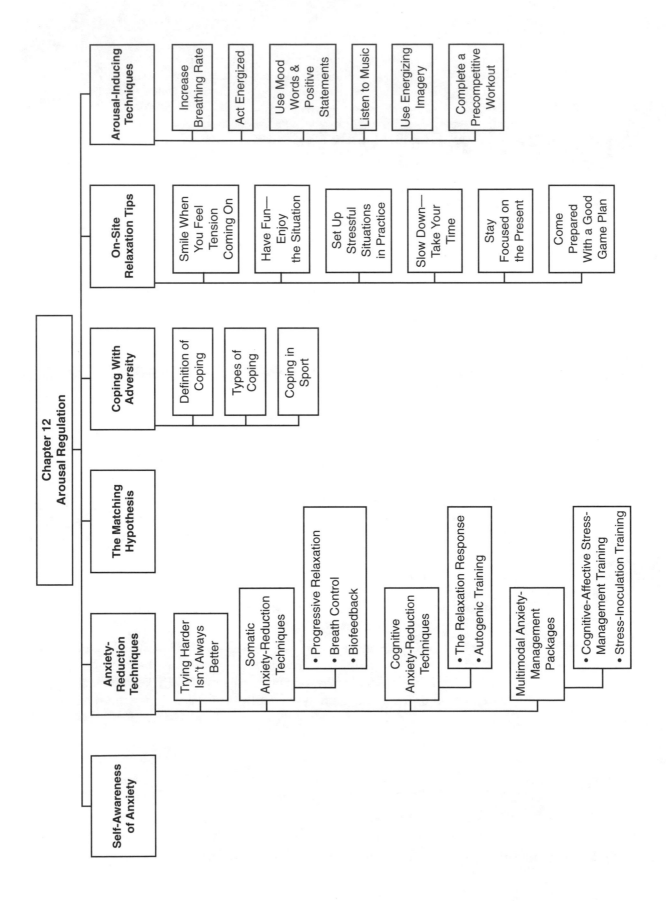

Chapter 12
Arousal Regulation

Self-Awareness of Anxiety

Anxiety-Reduction Techniques
- Trying Harder Isn't Always Better
- Somatic Anxiety-Reduction Techniques
  - Progressive Relaxation
  - Breath Control
  - Biofeedback
- Cognitive Anxiety-Reduction Techniques
  - The Relaxation Response
  - Autogenic Training
- Multimodal Anxiety-Management Packages
  - Cognitive-Affective Stress-Management Training
  - Stress-Inoculation Training

The Matching Hypothesis

Coping With Adversity
- Definition of Coping
- Types of Coping
- Coping in Sport

On-Site Relaxation Tips
- Smile When You Feel Tension Coming On
- Have Fun—Enjoy the Situation
- Set Up Stressful Situations in Practice
- Slow Down—Take Your Time
- Stay Focused on the Present
- Come Prepared With a Good Game Plan

Arousal-Inducing Techniques
- Increase Breathing Rate
- Act Energized
- Use Mood Words & Positive Statements
- Listen to Music
- Use Energizing Imagery
- Complete a Precompetitive Workout

Activity 12.1

Competitive Reflections

Do this activity after reading chapter 12 of *Foundations of Sport and Exercise Psychology*.

Directions: Considering the following questions will help you reflect on your personal competitive history, and develop or refine a precompetition plan as well as a competition focus plan. Analyzing your answers to the questions will help you increase your self-awareness of how your thoughts and feelings influence your performance, and how you can use mental skills in your sport. Be as honest as possible when answering. If something is unclear, please ask your instructor.

Think of your all-time best performance and respond to the following questions with that event in mind. (Adapted from Orlick, 1986.)

1. How did you feel just before the event? (Circle a number from 0 to 10.)

   No activation   Highly activated
   (mentally and physically flat)   (mentally and physically charged)

   0   1   2   3   4   5   6   7   8   9   10

   Not at all worried or scared   Extremely worried or scared

   0   1   2   3   4   5   6   7   8   9   10

2. What were you saying to yourself or thinking shortly before the start of the event?

3. How were you focused during the event (i.e., what were you aware of or paying attention to while actively engaged in the competition)?

Now think of your worst competitive performance and respond to the following questions with that event in mind.

4. How did you feel just before the event? (Circle a number from 0 to 10.)

   No activation   Highly activated
   (mentally and physically flat)   (mentally and physically charged)

   0   1   2   3   4   5   6   7   8   9   10

   Not at all worried or scared   Extremely worried or scared

   0   1   2   3   4   5   6   7   8   9   10

5. What were you saying to yourself or thinking shortly before the start of the event?

6. How were you focused during the event (i.e., what were you aware of or paying attention to while actively engaged in the competition)?

Study your responses to the above six questions before responding to the following.

7. What were the major differences between your thinking (or feeling) prior to your best and worst performances?

8. What were the major differences in your focus of attention between your best and worst performances?

9. How would you prefer to feel just before an important competition? (Circle a number from 0 to 10.)

No activation   Highly activated
(mentally and physically flat)   (mentally and physically charged)

0   1   2   3   4   5   6   7   8   9   10

Not at all worried or scared   Extremely worried or scared

0   1   2   3   4   5   6   7   8   9   10

10. How would you prefer to focus your attention during an important competition?

11. Is there anything you would change about the way you approach a competition?

12. Is there anything you would change about the way you approach practice and training?

13. Is there anything you would change about the way your coach approaches you (a) during practice and (b) during competition?

| Activity 12.2 | **Problem- Versus Emotion-Focused Coping** |

Do this activity after reading pages 258 to 259 of *Foundations of Sport and Exercise Psychology*.

Directions: Coping is a process of constantly changing cognitive and behavioral efforts to manage specific external and/or internal demands or conflicts appraised as taxing or exceeding one's resources. Coping can be classified into two types: problem-focused coping and emotion-focused coping. Problem-focused coping involves efforts to manage the problem that is causing the stress for the individual, and emotion-focused coping involves efforts to regulate the emotional responses to the problem that causes stress for the individual. Classify each of the following coping strategies as problem-focused coping (P) or emotion-focused coping (E).

_____ 1. A college gymnast reads ahead in her textbook to reduce the stress of trying to keep up in class during a heavy athletic travel schedule.

_____ 2. A basketball player takes a deep breath to relax before shooting a foul shot.

_____ 3. A coach sees a financial planner to come up with a plan for more effectively paying his bills, thus reducing the stress he experiences from being broke all the time.

_____ 4. A stockbroker starts an exercise program to deal with the stress of her job.

_____ 5. A physical educator restructures his teaching schedule to allow enough time to not be rushed getting to his after-school coaching duties.

Activity 12.3

Do this activity after reading chapter 12 of _Foundations of Sport and Exercise Psychology._

Relaxation Training Self-Evaluation

Directions: Read aloud and tape record the progressive relaxation script found on pages 250-251 of the textbook. Play the tape and follow the relaxation instructions. After completing the relaxation training session, answer these questions:

1. How long did your relaxation session last?

2. On a scale of 1 to 10 (1 = tense and 10 = extremely relaxed), how relaxed did you feel at the beginning of the session? _____ At the end of the session? _____

3. How well did your session go?

4. Identify ways the following exercise and sport science professionals could use relaxation training.

   Physical educator:

   Athletic trainer or physical therapist:

   Fitness instructor:

   Coach:

Answers to Selected Chapter 12 Activities

Activity 12.2:   Problem- Versus Emotion-Focused Coping

1. Problem-focused coping
2. Emotion-focused coping
3. Problem-focused coping
4. Emotion-focused coping
5. Problem-focused coping

Imagery

concepts

- Imagery refers to creating or recreating an experience in the mind and is affected by both situational and personal factors, such as the nature of the task, the skill level of the performer, and the imagery ability of the person.

- Novice and highly skilled performers who use imagery on cognitive tasks show the most positive effects.

- Traditional imagery theories contend that imagery works by producing muscle activity (psychoneuromuscular theory), providing a mental blueprint (symbolic learning theory), or improving other psychological skills like confidence (psychological skills hypothesis). More recent theories contend that both stimulus and response propositions of the image must be emphasized (bioinformational theory), and stress the importance of emphasizing the image itself, the somatic response of the image, and the meaning of the image (triple code model).

- There are two types of imagery: internal (imagining the execution of a skill from your own vantage point), and external (imagining yourself from the perspective of an external observer). Performers do not need to use only one or the other. To be most effective both types of imagery must involve not only the visual sense but also kinesthetic, auditory, tactile, and olfactory senses.

- Imagery can be used before and after practice and competition, during breaks in action, and during personal time. Imagery can also benefit the process of injury rehabilitation.

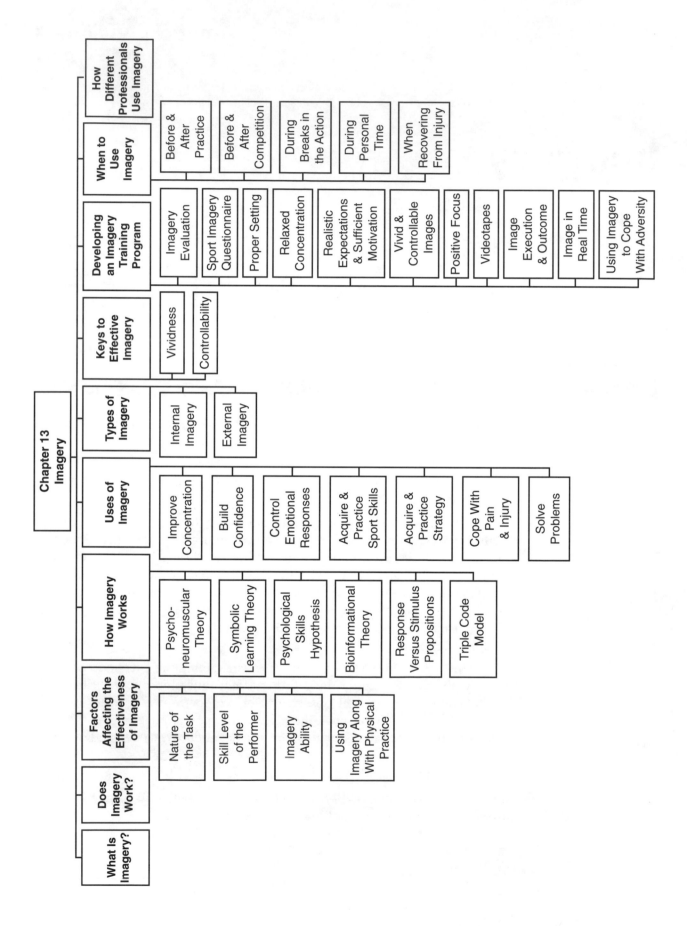

Chapter 13 Imagery

What Is Imagery?

Does Imagery Work?

Factors Affecting the Effectiveness of Imagery
- Nature of the Task
- Skill Level of the Performer
- Imagery Ability
- Using Imagery Along With Physical Practice

How Imagery Works
- Psycho-neuromuscular Theory
- Symbolic Learning Theory
- Psychological Skills Hypothesis
- Bioinformational Theory
- Response Versus Stimulus Propositions
- Triple Code Model

Uses of Imagery
- Improve Concentration
- Build Confidence
- Control Emotional Responses
- Acquire & Practice Sport Skills
- Acquire & Practice Strategy
- Cope With Pain & Injury
- Solve Problems

Types of Imagery
- Internal Imagery
- External Imagery

Keys to Effective Imagery
- Vividness
- Controllability

Developing an Imagery Training Program
- Imagery Evaluation
- Sport Imagery Questionnaire
- Proper Setting
- Relaxed Concentration
- Realistic Expectations & Sufficient Motivation
- Vivid & Controllable Images
- Positive Focus
- Videotapes
- Image Execution & Outcome
- Image in Real Time
- Using Imagery to Cope With Adversity

When to Use Imagery
- Before & After Practice
- Before & After Competition
- During Breaks in the Action
- During Personal Time
- When Recovering From Injury

How Different Professionals Use Imagery

| Activity 13.1 | Imagery Vividness |

Do this activity after reading chapter 13 of *Foundations of Sport and Exercise Psychology*.

Directions: As your instructor reads the following imagery scenario (or after you read it), imagine that you are in this situation executing the skills required. After you produce the image, rate its vividness by circling the numbers that best correspond to the descriptions of your image. Write any comments in the space provided. (Reprinted from ACEP, 1987.)

Sport Arena Imagery Scenario: Imagine yourself walking out of the locker room and into a pool area. Notice the change in temperature and humidity. Take a deep breath and smell the chlorination. As you walk, notice the feel of the pool deck. Is it rough? Smooth? Slippery? Now look around the pool. Look at the gallery, the record boards, and the banners hanging from the wall. In your mind's eye, create an image of the competition pool. Imagine the starting blocks, the colors of the lane lines, the flags over the pool. Now see yourself warming up in the pool. Feel the cool water against your skin as you move through the water. Hear your teammates and fans talking and cheering. Finally, focus on the feelings you have as you move around the swimming pool.

Vividness Ratings:	Low				High
Overall vividness	1	2	3	4	5
Sight vividness	1	2	3	4	5
Touch vividness	1	2	3	4	5
Sound vividness	1	2	3	4	5
Emotional vividness	1	2	3	4	5

Comments:

| Activity 13.2 | Imagery Control  |

Do this activity after reading chapter 13 of *Foundations of Sport and Exercise Psychology*.

Directions: As your instructor reads the imagery scenario (or after you read it), imagine that you are in this situation executing the skills as required. After you produce the image, rate your control over the image by circling the number that best corresponds to the description of your image. Write comments you have on the exercise in the space provided. (Reprinted from ACEP, 1987.)

Ice Water Imagery Scenario: Imagine that you have twisted your ankle. You know you need to get some ice onto the injury to reduce the swelling. Feel the throbbing in your foot and ankle. Now imagine gingerly putting your foot into a bucket of ice water. Feel the cold sensation. You're tempted to remove your foot from the ice mixture as the coldness grows to a burning sensation. And your foot is very cold. Feel the coldness and toughness of your flesh. As time passes, your foot moves from feeling cold to feeling numb. Focus on these sensations. Your ice treatment is now over. Imagine yourself taking your foot out of the bucket. Immediately your foot begins to regain feeling. You feel the burning sensation. Now you feel extreme cold in your toes. Gradually, however, you begin to feel the warmth radiating from your ankle down into your toes. Tell yourself that your foot is now completely warm again.

Control Ratings:	Low				High
Start and stop images on command	1	2	3	4	5
Make images do what you want them to	1	2	3	4	5

Comments:

Activity 13.3

Do this activity after reading chapter 13 of *Foundations of Sport and Exercise Psychology*.

Sport Imagery Questionnaire

Directions: As your instructor reads the following four imagery situations, imagine each general situation and provide as much detail from your imagination as possible to make the image seem real. You will then be asked to rate your imagery in these five ways:

- How vividly you saw or visualized the image
- How clearly you heard the sounds
- How vividly you felt your body movements
- How clearly you were aware of your state of mind or mood or felt the emotions of the situation
- How well you were able to control the images

Now close your eyes and take a few deep breaths to become as relaxed as you can. Put aside all other thoughts. Keep your eyes closed and try to imagine the situation described. Be sure to think of specific examples of the skill, the people involved, the place, the time, and so on. There are, of course, no right or wrong images. However, your accurate appraisal of your images will help you determine what aspects of imagery you need to focus on in the development of your imagery skills. After imagining each situation, rate the five dimensions by circling the appropriate response: 1 = Very poor, 2 = Poor, 3 = Moderate, 4 = Well, and 5 = Very well. (Adapted from ACEP, 1987.)

Situation 1: Select a specific skill or situation in your sport. Imagine yourself performing the activity in the place where you would normally practice, without anyone else present. Now close your eyes for about a minute. Try to see yourself at this place: hear the sounds, feel the body movements, and be aware of your mood.

1. Rate how well you saw yourself performing the activity.	1	2	3	4	5
2. Rate how well you heard the sounds.	1	2	3	4	5
3. Rate how well you felt yourself performing the activity.	1	2	3	4	5
4. Rate how well you were aware of your mood.	1	2	3	4	5
5. Rate how well you controlled your image.	1	2	3	4	5

Situation 2: You are performing the same activity as in Situation 1, but this time the coach and your teammates are present. You make a mistake that everyone notices. Now close your eyes for about a minute and imagine making the error and what occurs immediately afterward.

1. Rate how well you saw yourself.	1	2	3	4	5
2. Rate how well you heard the sounds.	1	2	3	4	5
3. Rate how well you felt yourself making the movements.	1	2	3	4	5
4. Rate how well you felt the emotions.	1	2	3	4	5
5. Rate how well you controlled your image.	1	2	3	4	5

Situation 3: Think of a teammate performing a specific activity unsuccessfully in a contest (e.g., missing a 20-foot shot, being passed by other runners, falling from the balance beam, missing a field goal.) Now close your eyes for about a minute to imagine watching your teammate performing this activity unsuccessfully in a critical part of the contest as vividly and realistically as possible.

1. Rate how well you saw your teammate.	1	2	3	4	5
2. Rate how well you heard the sounds.	1	2	3	4	5
3. Rate how well you felt your own physical presence or movement.	1	2	3	4	5
4. Rate how well you felt your own emotions.	1	2	3	4	5
5. Rate how well you controlled your image.	1	2	3	4	5

Situation 4: Imagine yourself performing the same activity that you imagined your teammate performing in Situation 3. Imagine yourself performing the activity very skillfully. Spectators and teammates show their appreciation. Now close your eyes for about a minute and imagine the situation as vividly as possible.

1. Rate how well you saw yourself.	1	2	3	4	5
2. Rate how well you heard the sounds.	1	2	3	4	5
3. Rate how well you felt yourself making the movements.	1	2	3	4	5
4. Rate how well you felt the emotions.	1	2	3	4	5
5. Rate how well you controlled your image.	1	2	3	4	5

Now add up your responses to each question and write your scores in the spaces provided.

Dimension Score

Visual (total your scores for Question 1) = _____

Auditory (total your scores for Question 2) = _____

Kinesthetic (total your scores for Question 3) = _____

Mood (total your scores for Question 4) = _____

Control (total your scores for Question 5) = _____

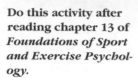

Activity 13.4

Test Your Imagery Timing

Do this activity after reading chapter 13 of *Foundations of Sport and Exercise Psychology*.

Directions: Think of a sport or physical activity that you have some experience with (e.g., swimming 50 meters freestyle; starting from half-court, dribble for a lay-up). Perform the activity while someone times how long it takes you to perform. At a later time, lie down at home and imagine yourself doing the same activity. Time yourself to see determine how close your imagined and actual performance imagery times were.

_____ Actual performance time

_____ Imagery performance time

Activity 13.5

"Visualization: What You See Is What You Get"—Video Analysis

Do this activity after reading chapter 13 of *Foundations of Sport and Exercise Psychology*.

Directions: As you watch the video "Visualization: What You See Is What You Get" (Coaching Association of Canada), record your answers to the following questions on a separate sheet of paper:

1. How do people use visualization?

2. What are the advantages of using visualization?

3. What are some terms that might help people use visualization?

4. What tips or guidelines might help people in developing their visualization skills?

Answers to Selected Chapter 13 Activities

Activity 13.5: "Visualization: What You See Is What You Get"—Video Analysis

1. Among other things, people can use visualization to help prepare mentally for practice, to prepare mentally for a game, to correct errors, to practice behavior, to get into flow, to simulate good game and practice partners, to facilitate injury rehabilitation, and to help anticipate what to expect in game situations.

2. Visualization can be used during the off-season and when people are fatigued or injured.

3. (a) Power of the mind's eye; (b) "Can you see yourself?"; (c) Visualizing is not daydreaming; (d) What the mind sees, the mind believes and your heart can achieve.

4. (a) Practice visualization and use it every day; (b) Include positive affirmation in imagery scripts; (c) Feel the skills; (d) Move slightly when performing imagery exercise; (e) The more descriptive the image, the better; (f) Test and monitor your imagery skills; (g) Start alone in a quiet environment, then move to noisy places; (h) Start with skills you can use, then move to more competitive skills; (i) Simulate competitive pressure.

Self-Confidence

concepts

- Self-confidence is the belief that one can successfully perform a desired behavior. High levels of confidence can enhance positive emotions, facilitate concentration, move one to set more challenging goals, increase effort, and develop effective competitive strategies.

- Self and other expectations have been repeatedly shown to influence performance. Coach/instructor expectations are particularly powerful and affect athlete/student performance via four steps: (1) coaches form expectations; (2) coaches' expectations influence their own behavior; (3) coaches' behaviors affect athletes' performances; and (4) athletes' performances confirm the coaches' expectations.

- Self-efficacy is the perception of one's ability to perform a particular task successfully and is a situation-specific form of self-confidence. Sources of self-efficacy include performance accomplishments, vicarious experiences, verbal persuasion, imaginal experiences, physiological states, and emotional states.

- Modeling or demonstrations can best be understood through a four-stage process: attention; retention; motor reproduction; and motivation.

- Strategies for enhancing one's self-confidence include acting confidently, thinking confidently, using imagery, being in good physical condition, and preparing mentally and physically for upcoming performances.

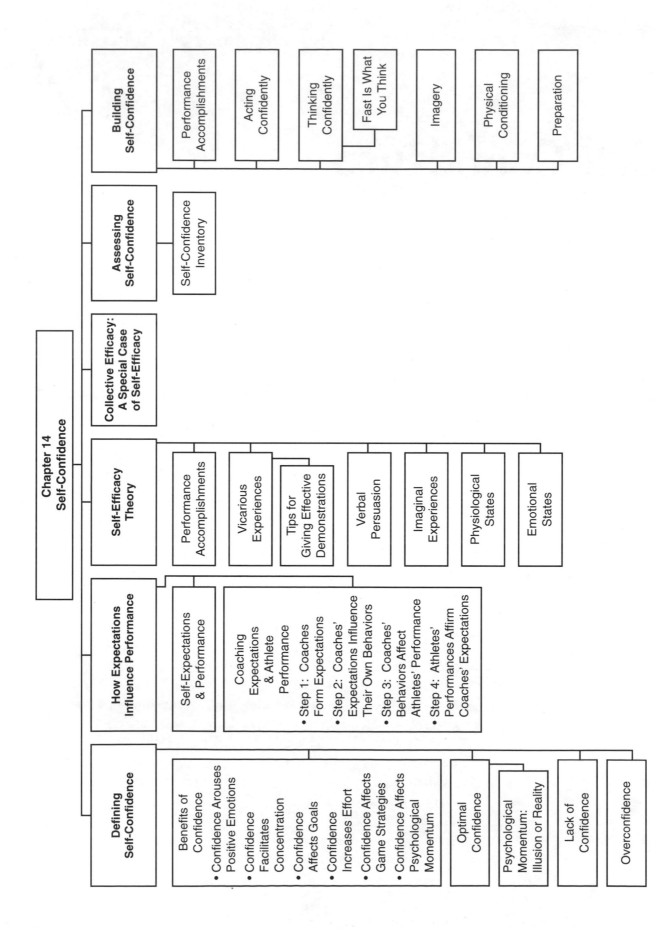

**Chapter 14
Self-Confidence**

**Defining
Self-Confidence**

Benefits of
Confidence

- Confidence Arouses
  Positive Emotions
- Confidence
  Facilitates
  Concentration
- Confidence
  Affects Goals
- Confidence
  Increases Effort
- Confidence Affects
  Game Strategies
- Confidence Affects
  Psychological
  Momentum

Optimal
Confidence

Psychological
Momentum:
Illusion or Reality

Lack of
Confidence

Overconfidence

**How Expectations
Influence Performance**

Self-Expectations
& Performance

Coaching
Expectations
& Athlete
Performance

- Step 1: Coaches
  Form Expectations
- Step 2: Coaches'
  Expectations Influence
  Their Own Behaviors
- Step 3: Coaches'
  Behaviors Affect
  Athletes' Performance
- Step 4: Athletes'
  Performances Affirm
  Coaches' Expectations

**Self-Efficacy
Theory**

Performance
Accomplishments

Vicarious
Experiences

Tips for
Giving Effective
Demonstrations

Verbal
Persuasion

Imaginal
Experiences

Physiological
States

Emotional
States

**Collective Efficacy:
A Special Case
of Self-Efficacy**

**Assessing
Self-Confidence**

Self-Confidence
Inventory

**Building
Self-Confidence**

Performance
Accomplishments

Acting
Confidently

Thinking
Confidently

Fast Is What
You Think

Imagery

Physical
Conditioning

Preparation

Enhancing Self-Efficacy

Do this activity after reading pages 292 to 298 of *Foundations of Sport and Exercise Psychology.*

Directions: This exercise helps you identify ways to enhance the self-efficacy or confidence of your students, athletes, or clients. As discussed in the text, information about an individual's self-confidence comes from one of the six sources listed below. Divide into groups, and identify for each source three or four ways to increase self-efficacy. Use situation-specific examples from your professional setting (e.g., physical education class, sport team, cardiac rehabilitation setting, etc.).

1. Performance accomplishments:

2. Vicarious experience (modeling):

3. Verbal persuasion:

4. Emotional arousal:

5. Physiological state:

6. Imaginal experiences:

Assessing Self-Confidence

Do this activity after reading chapter 14 of *Foundations of Sport and Exercise Psychology.*

Directions: Read each question carefully and think about your confidence regarding each item during competition. For each item, indicate the percentage of time you feel you had either too little, too much, or just the right degree of confidence.

For example, you are a pole-vaulter. How confident are you each time you attempt to clear 17 feet? (Adapted from ACEP, 1987.)

Underconfident	**Confident**	**Overconfident**
20%	70%	10%

Note. The three answers should always add up to 100%. Distribute this 100% however you feel is appropriate; you may assign all 100% to one category, split it between two categories, or, as in the example, divide it among three categories.

How confident are you with respect to:

1. Your ability to execute the skills of your sport or exercise?

Underconfident	**Confident**	**Overconfident**
%	%	%

2. Your ability to make critical decisions during the contest?

Underconfident	**Confident**	**Overconfident**
%	%	%

3. Your ability to concentrate?

Underconfident	Confident	Overconfident
%	%	%

4. Your ability to perform under pressure?

Underconfident	Confident	Overconfident
%	%	%

5. Your ability to execute successful strategy?

Underconfident	Confident	Overconfident
%	%	%

6. Your ability to put forth the effort needed to succeed?

Underconfident	Confident	Overconfident
%	%	%

7. Your ability to control your emotions during competition?

Underconfident	Confident	Overconfident
%	%	%

8. Your physical conditioning or training?

Underconfident	Confident	Overconfident
%	%	%

9. Your ability to relate successfully with your coach?

Underconfident	Confident	Overconfident
%	%	%

10. Your ability to come back from behind?

Underconfident	Confident	Overconfidentt
%	%	%

Answers to Selected Chapter 14 Activities

Activity 14.1:   Enhancing Self-Efficacy

For a middle school physical education class

1. I would scale activities so that success can be achieved by individuals of various skill levels; I would have the students fill out skill cards with checks or stickers for each step a student achieves.

2. I would show a video with popular athletes demonstrating the skill; I would bring in students who successfully learned the skill in the previous year.

3. I would focus on being aware of individual student strengths—and remind the students of these strengths often; I would encourage classmates to positively encourage one another; I would help students learn to remind themselves of their strengths and abilities.

4. I would focus on reframing nervousness to excitement in the gym; I would explain the importance and benefits of emotional arousal.

5. I would have the students practice relaxed breathing before attempting new skills; I would use consistent cue words to remind students to remain relaxed.

6. I would teach imagery sensory awareness that would allow students to mentally practice the new skills.

Goal Setting

concepts

- Goals are objectives or aims of actions. They may be subjective or objective, and they may be directed toward performance (self-comparisons for improvement), process (actions that lead to improved performance), or outcome (beating or surpassing others).

- Specific goals, as compared to general "do-your-best" goals, are most effective for producing behavioral change.

- Goals influence behavior "directly" by focusing a performer's attention on important elements of the skill or task, increasing motivation and persistence, and facilitating the development of new learning strategies. Goals also influence behavior "indirectly" by causing changes in important psychological factors, such as self-confidence, anxiety, and satisfaction.

- Basic goal-setting principles include: set specific goals; set moderately difficult but realistic goals; set long- and short-term goals; set performance and process, as well as outcome goals; set practice and competition goals; record goals; develop goal-achievement strategies; consider the participant's personality and motivation; foster an individual's goal commitment; provide goal support; and provide evaluation and feedback about goals.

- Common goal-setting problems that a good program must address include: failing to convince students, athletes, and exercisers to set goals; failing to set specific goals; setting too many goals too soon; failing to adjust goals flexibly as the situation requires; failing to set performance and process goals; and not initiating goal-setting follow-up and evaluation.

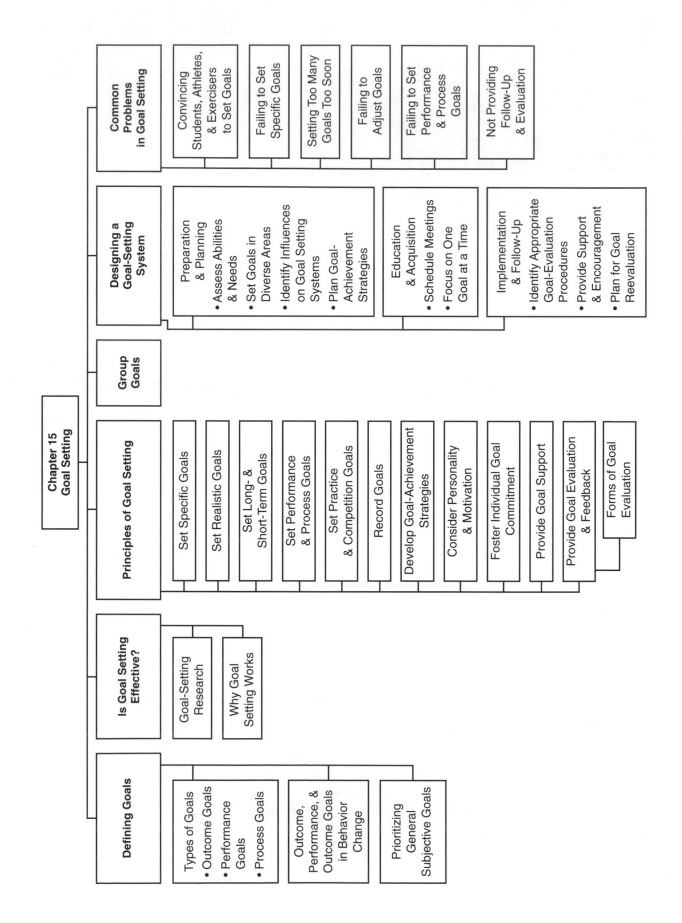

**Chapter 15
Goal Setting**

Defining Goals

Types of Goals
• Outcome Goals
• Performance Goals
• Process Goals

Outcome, Performance, & Outcome Goals in Behavior Change

Prioritizing General Subjective Goals

Is Goal Setting Effective?

Goal-Setting Research

Why Goal Setting Works

Principles of Goal Setting

Set Specific Goals

Set Realistic Goals

Set Long- & Short-Term Goals

Set Performance & Process Goals

Set Practice & Competition Goals

Record Goals

Develop Goal-Achievement Strategies

Consider Personality & Motivation

Foster Individual Goal Commitment

Provide Goal Support

Provide Goal Evaluation & Feedback

Forms of Goal Evaluation

Group Goals

Designing a Goal-Setting System

Preparation & Planning
• Assess Abilities & Needs
• Set Goals in Diverse Areas
• Identify Influences on Goal Setting Systems
• Plan Goal-Achievement Strategies

Education & Acquisition
• Schedule Meetings
• Focus on One Goal at a Time

Implementation & Follow-Up
• Identify Appropriate Goal-Evaluation Procedures
• Provide Support & Encouragement
• Plan for Goal Reevaluation

Common Problems in Goal Setting

Convincing Students, Athletes, & Exercisers to Set Goals

Failing to Set Specific Goals

Setting Too Many Goals Too Soon

Failing to Adjust Goals

Failing to Set Performance & Process Goals

Not Providing Follow-Up & Evaluation

| Activity 15.1 |

Examining Your Goals

Do this activity after reading chapter 15 of *Foundations of Sport and Exercise Psychology*.

Directions: Complete the questions below based on either your athletic experience, exercise interests, or professional-career goals (e.g., to become a physical therapist). (Adapted from Orlick, 1986.)

1. Dream goal (long-term): What is your long-term dream goal? What is possible in the long-term if you stretch all your limits?

2. Dream goal (this year): What is your dream goal for this year? What is possible if you stretch all your limits this year?

3. Realistic performance goal (this year): What is a realistic performance goal that you can achieve this year, based on your present skill level, your potential for improvement, and your current motivation?

4. Monthly goal: Set a personal goal that you feel you can achieve within the next month. Name one goal you would like to focus on with special intensity.

5. Next class or practice goal: Set a personal goal that you feel you can achieve by the end of your next class or practice. Name one goal you would like to focus on with special intensity.

Goal-Setting Reminders

- Goals should be specific, challenging, and realistic.
- Focus on performance goals before outcome goals.
- Set game goals and practice goals.
- Write down your goals so you can see them daily.
- Evaluate your goals as you make progress.

| Activity 15.2 |

Prioritizing Your Subjective Goals

Do this activity after reading chapter 15 of *Foundations of Sport and Exercise Psychology*.

Directions: Subjective goals are general statements of intent (e.g., "Do well in school," "hold a job and make money," "graduate"). In this exercise you are to think about and identify the most important general subjective goals that you now hold. Then you will prioritize each of your subjective goals.

General subjective goals:

1. _____
   _____

2. _____
   _____

3. _____
   _____

4. _____
   _____
5. _____
   _____
6. _____
   _____

Goal prioritization:

Reflect on the goals you identified above and then prioritize them, with "A" being most important, "B" being somewhat important, and "C" being less important. Please note that you cannot rate all your goals as A (use at least one B and C).

Activity 15.3

Do this activity after reading chapter 15 of *Foundations of Sport and Exercise Psychology*.

Analyzing Your Goals

Directions: List five of your goals for exercise or athletic experiences.

Goals:

1. _____
   _____
2. _____
   _____
3. _____
   _____
4. _____
   _____
5. _____
   _____

Goal-setting principles:

Now rate these goals on each of the goal-setting principles listed below by placing a checkmark in the appropriate column if your goal conforms to that principle. (Adapted from ACEP, 1987.)

	Performance	Realistic	Specific	Short-term	Individual
1.	____	____	____	____	____
2.	____	____	____	____	____
3.	____	____	____	____	____
4.	____	____	____	____	____
5.	____	____	____	____	____

Based on the above analysis, what are your goal-setting strengths and weaknesses?

Strengths:

Weaknesses:

Climbing the Mountain of Behavioral Change

Do this activity after reading chapter 15 of *Foundations of Sport and Exercise Psychology*.

Directions: Determine a terminal goal that you would like to achieve (e.g., become a head coach, graduate with honors, break into the starting line-up). Place it on the top of the mountain of behavioral change shown below. Then list three short-term goals that will move you toward achieving your long-term terminal goal.

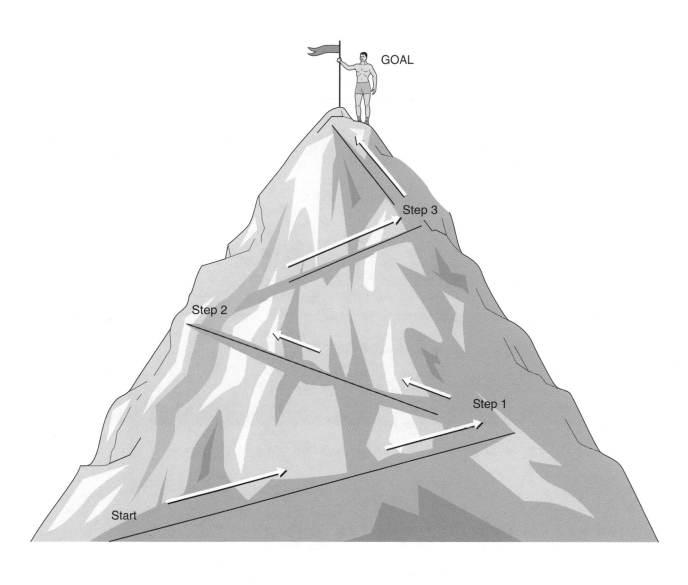

GOAL

Step 3

Step 2

Step 1

Start

1. _____

2. _____

3. _____

| Activity 15.5 | **Overcoming Common Goal-Setting Problems** |

Do this activity after reading chapter 15 of *Foundations of Sport and Exercise Psychology.*

Directions: Think about the goals you set in activity 15.4. Indicate which of the problems listed below you feel you will encounter in achieving the goals you have identified by circling "yes" if you think you will experience difficulty, "no" if you do not foresee having a problem. Next, identify at least one strategy you could use to avoid or overcome the identified problem.

Problem	**Will experience problem?**	
Convincing yourself to actually set goals	Yes	No
Strategy for overcoming or avoiding problem:		
Failing to set specific goals	Yes	No
Strategy for overcoming or avoiding problem:		
Setting too many goals too soon	Yes	No
Strategy for overcoming or avoiding problem:		
Failing to adjust goals	Yes	No
Strategy for overcoming or avoiding problem:		
Failing to set performance and process goals	Yes	No
Strategy for overcoming or avoiding problem:		
Not providing for follow-up and evaluation	Yes	No
Strategy for overcoming or avoiding problem:		

Answers to Selected Chapter 15 Activities

Activity 15.4:   Climbing the Mountain of Behavioral Change

Terminal goal: Making the high school tennis team.

Start—Weeks 1-4: Jog 2-3 times per week for 30 minutes. Weightlift 3 times per week for 40 minutes.

Step 1—Weeks 5-6: Jog 2 times per week for 20 minutes. Weightlift 3 times per week for 40 minutes. Practice basic tennis skills 3 days per week for 1 hour.

Step 2—Weeks 7-8: Jog 2 times per week for 20 minutes. Weightlift 3 times per week for 40 minutes. Practice basic tennis skills 2 days per week for 1 hour. Work on ground stroke consistency 3 days per week for 1 hour.

Step 3—Weeks 9-10: Jog 2 times per week for 20 minutes. Weightlift 2 times per week for 40 minutes. Practice basic tennis skills and ground stroke consistency 3 days per week for 1 hour. Work on serve and volley consistency 3 days per week for 1 hour. Play 1 match per week.

Step 4—Weeks 11-12: Jog 2 times per week for 20 minutes. Weightlift 2 times per week for 40 minutes. Practice basic tennis skills and ground stroke consistency 3 days per week for 1 hour. Work on serve and volley consistency 3 days per week for 1 hour. Play 2 matches per week. Have a good tryout.

Concentration

concepts

- Concentration involves focusing on relevant cues in the environment, maintaining the focus over time, and being aware of the changing situation.

- Four different types of attentional focus have been identified: broad-external; narrow-external; broad-internal; and narrow-internal. Different tasks or sports require different types of attention for effective performance.

- Attentional problems can be categorized as coming from internal sources (e.g., attending to past events, overanalyzing body mechanics) or external sources (e.g., audience, crowd noise).

- Effective attenders can attend to several stimuli without getting overloaded and can narrow attentional focus without leaving out important information. Ineffective attenders are easily confused by multiple stimuli.

- Self-talk takes many forms, but it can be simply categorized as positive and negative. Positive self-talk is an asset that can enhance self-esteem, motivation, and attentional focus. Negative self-talk is critical and self-demeaning, and it tends to produce anxiety, which undermines concentration.

- Routines can be used before or during an event to focus attention, reduce anxiety, eliminate distractions, and enhance confidence.

- Concentration can be improved by using simulations, employing instructional or informational cues words, using nonjudgmental thinking, developing competitive plans, and establishing routines.

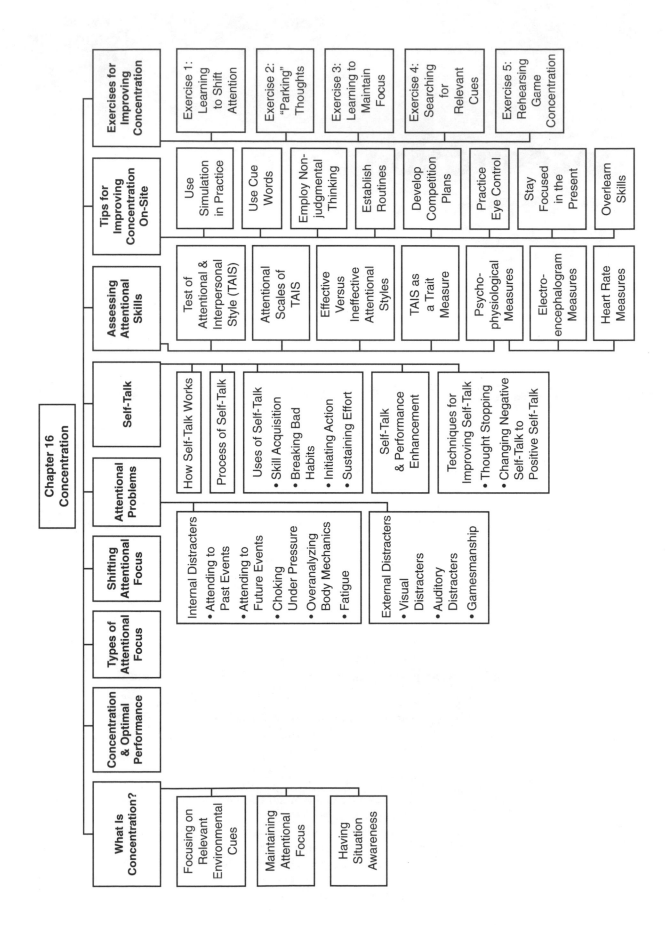

Chapter 16: Concentration

- **What Is Concentration?**
  - Focusing on Relevant Environmental Cues
  - Maintaining Attentional Focus
  - Having Situation Awareness

- **Concentration & Optimal Performance**

- **Types of Attentional Focus**

- **Shifting Attentional Focus**

- **Attentional Problems**
  - Internal Distracters
    - Attending to Past Events
    - Attending to Future Events
    - Choking Under Pressure
    - Overanalyzing Body Mechanics
    - Fatigue
  - External Distracters
    - Visual Distracters
    - Auditory Distracters
    - Gamesmanship

- **Self-Talk**
  - How Self-Talk Works
  - Process of Self-Talk
  - Uses of Self-Talk
    - Skill Acquisition
    - Breaking Bad Habits
    - Initiating Action
    - Sustaining Effort
  - Self-Talk & Performance Enhancement
  - Techniques for Improving Self-Talk
    - Thought Stopping
    - Changing Negative Self-Talk to Positive Self-Talk

- **Assessing Attentional Skills**
  - Test of Attentional & Interpersonal Style (TAIS)
  - Attentional Scales of TAIS
  - Effective Versus Ineffective Attentional Styles
  - TAIS as a Trait Measure
  - Psycho-physiological Measures
  - Electro-encephalogram Measures
  - Heart Rate Measures

- **Tips for Improving Concentration On-Site**
  - Use Simulation in Practice
  - Use Cue Words
  - Employ Non-judgmental Thinking
  - Establish Routines
  - Develop Competition Plans
  - Practice Eye Control
  - Stay Focused in the Present
  - Overlearn Skills

- **Exercises for Improving Concentration**
  - Exercise 1: Learning to Shift Attention
  - Exercise 2: "Parking" Thoughts
  - Exercise 3: Learning to Maintain Focus
  - Exercise 4: Searching for Relevant Cues
  - Exercise 5: Rehearsing Game Concentration

Activity 16.1

Thought Stopping

Do this activity after reading chapter 16 of *Foundations of Sport and Exercise Psychology*.

Directions: Select a sport or exercise activity situation (e.g., making a shot over the water in golf, getting up early in the morning to exercise) where you typically find yourself thinking negatively. Complete the following worksheet to identify the specific nature of your negative thoughts and replace them with positive thoughts. (Adapted from ACEP, 1987.)

1. Describe the situation as completely as possible:

2. Identify the negative self-statements you make in this particular situation:

3. Specify a term or cue that you will use as a signal to stop your negative thoughts:

4. List four realistic, positive, and constructive self-statements that you can use to replace the negative thoughts:

Activity 16.2

Changing From Negative to Positive Self-Talk

Do this activity after reading pages 336 to 338 of *Foundations of Sport and Exercise Psychology*.

Directions: Read the following case study and complete the worksheet to help George change his thoughts from negative to positive. (Adapted from ACEP, 1987.)

Case Study: George is a talented wrestler who over the course of his career has compiled a record of 40-11. At last year's sectional tournament, this is what happened:

As George weighed in, he saw his scheduled opponent, Jim, who attended a rival high school. Jim looked bigger and stronger than the usual competitors in George's weight class. George began to question whether Jim would even make weight. As the weigh-in continued, George learned that Jim did indeed make weight. In addition, he discovered that the only time Jim was defeated during the season was when he wrestled up a class. George began to think about Jim's size, how strong he looked, and his record.

At warm-ups, George began to question his own ability to wrestle against Jim. He watched Jim and dwelt on how strong and tough he looked. George began to think, "I can't possibly beat Jim. What will my friends and teammates think of me if I lose? If this guy is as strong as he looks, he might pin me. That would really be embarrassing."

These thoughts commanded George's attention. As a result, his warm-up was not particularly good. He moved off the mat with an uneasy feeling. Still he eyed Jim. As their match grew closer, Jim appeared to be relaxed and focused on the bout. George was still dwelling on Jim's size and strength and on the outcome of the match. He appeared distracted and expressed his worries.

Questions:

1. What are three negative statements George might have been making to himself?

2. How can you help George recognize these statements?

3. What positive self-statements could George make to dispute each of the negative statements?

   Negative Statement #1:

   Negative Statement #2:

   Negative Statement #3:

| Activity 16.3 | Concentration Grid |

Do this activity after reading pages 346 to 348 of *Foundations of Sport and Exercise Psychology*.

Directions: Ask a partner to time you for one minute. During that time, beginning with the number 00, put a slash through as many consecutive numbers as you can. (Reprinted from ACEP, 1987.)

84	27	51	78	59	52	13	85	61	55
28	60	92	04	97	90	31	57	29	33
32	96	65	39	80	77	49	86	18	70
76	87	71	95	98	81	01	46	88	00
48	82	89	47	35	17	10	42	62	34
44	67	93	11	07	43	72	94	69	56
53	79	05	22	54	74	58	14	91	02
06	68	99	75	26	15	41	66	20	40
50	09	64	08	38	30	36	45	83	24
03	73	21	23	16	37	25	19	12	63

> **Activity 16.4**

Developing a Concentration Routine

Do this activity after reading chapter 16 of *Foundations of Sport and Exercise Psychology*.

Directions: Select a sport skill that you have some experience performing (e.g., tennis serve, golf drive, basketball free throw) and develop a sport-specific routine for enhancing your concentration. Be sure to incorporate cue words and nonjudgmental thinking into your routine.

Sport/Activity:

Routine:

Now indicate how you might practice the selected sport skill and concentration routine in a simulated competitive environment.

Answers to Selected Chapter 16 Activities

Activity 16.1: Thought Stopping

1. I am trying to learn how to swim the length of the pool using the freestyle stroke. I am in a beginning swim class and can swim with my head out of the water. I am trying to learn to keep my head in the water and use the side-breathing technique, but I'm having a really hard time coordinating all of the movements.

2. a. I will never be able to do the breathing at the same time as everything else (moving my arms and legs).

   b. I am a terrible swimmer.

   c. Everyone else in my swimming class has already learned to do this; I must be a really slow learner.

   d. I hate putting my face in the water and getting water up my nose!

3. I am going to imagine my negative thoughts floating in the pool and being sucked down the drain.

4. a. Focus on feeling the flow . . . 1, 2, breathe . . . 1, 2, breathe.

   b. I am learning to swim—don't worry about everybody else.

   c. I am progressing at my own pace and show improvement with each lesson.

   d. I just need to blow bubbles out my nose each time I put my face in the water.

Activity 16.4:   Developing a Concentration Routine

Sport/Activity: Golf Swing

Routine:

1. Take a deep breath.

2. Check ball lie and assess weather conditions and possible hazards.

3. Look at target and decide on shot required.

4. Imagine target and shot—see ball trajectory.

5. Address ball and adjust body to ensure comfortable position.

6. Feel shot with whole body.

7. Think easy and swing.

Now indicate how you might practice the selected sport skill and concentration routine in a simulated competitive environment.

After practicing your concentration routine at the driving range, have a friend watch your swing and make negative comments, or have him or her click a camera shutter as you swing.

Enhancing Health and Well-Being

Exercise and Psychological Well-Being

concepts

- Exercise has been shown to be related to reductions in negative emotional states such as depression and anxiety, although a cause-effect relationship has not been established. Reduction in anxiety and depression are maximized with regular exercise of moderate intensity that is 20 to 30 minutes in duration, aerobic in nature, and enjoyable.

- Low-intensity aerobic and anaerobic exercise is related to changes in mood states, such as decreases in fatigue and anger and increases in vigor, alertness, and energy.

- The positive relationship between exercise and psychological well-being is explained by both psychological (e.g., feelings of competency and sense of control) and physiological (e.g., reductions in muscle tension, increases in blood flow) mechanisms.

- Changes in personality (e.g., increased self-confidence) and intelligence, as well as changes in cognitive functioning (e.g., attentional control) have been linked to increases in exercise.

- Positive addiction to exercise has been shown to be associated with positive psychological outcomes and increases in life satisfaction, but negative addiction to exercise (when exercise controls one's life) is associated with negative outcomes at home and work. For those negatively addicted to exercise, not being able to exercise can cause severe depression.

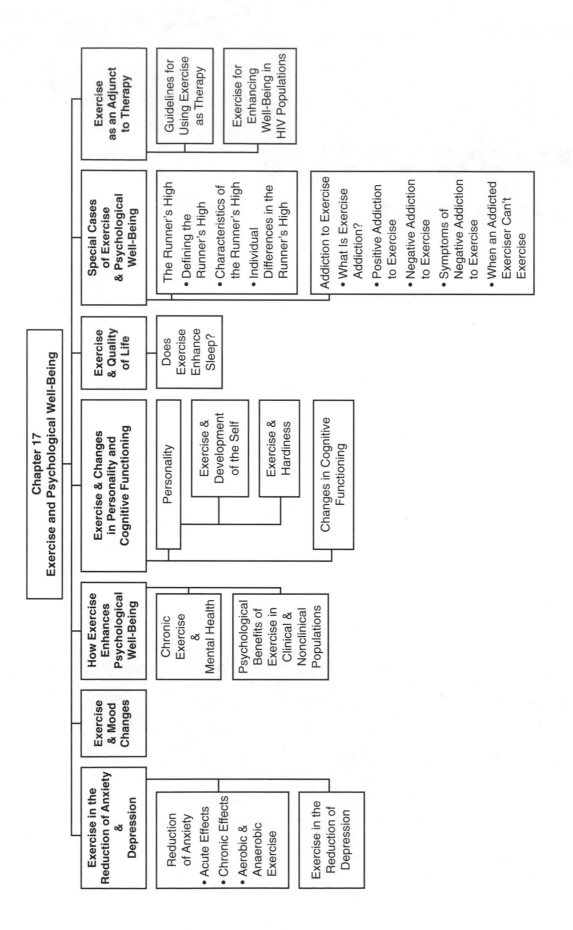

Chapter 17
Exercise and Psychological Well-Being

Exercise in the Reduction of Anxiety & Depression

Reduction of Anxiety
• Acute Effects
• Chronic Effects
• Aerobic & Anaerobic Exercise

Exercise in the Reduction of Depression

Exercise & Mood Changes

How Exercise Enhances Psychological Well-Being

Chronic Exercise & Mental Health

Psychological Benefits of Exercise in Clinical & Nonclinical Populations

Exercise & Changes in Personality and Cognitive Functioning

Personality

Exercise & Development of the Self

Exercise & Hardiness

Changes in Cognitive Functioning

Exercise & Quality of Life

Does Exercise Enhance Sleep?

Special Cases of Exercise & Psychological Well-Being

The Runner's High
• Defining the Runner's High
• Characteristics of the Runner's High
• Individual Differences in the Runner's High

Addiction to Exercise
• What Is Exercise Addiction?
• Positive Addiction to Exercise
• Negative Addiction to Exercise
• Symptoms of Negative Addiction to Exercise
• When an Addicted Exerciser Can't Exercise

Exercise as an Adjunct to Therapy

Guidelines for Using Exercise as Therapy

Exercise for Enhancing Well-Being in HIV Populations

Activity 17.1	# Exercise and Psychological Well-Being Survey

Do this activity after reading chapter 17 of *Foundations of Sport and Exercise Psychology.*

Directions: Based on your exercise experiences, complete the following questions.

1. Do you exercise regularly (at least 3 times a week for 20 to 30 minutes)?

2. a. Do you feel better after you exercise?

    b. If "Yes" to question 2a, check the ways you feel better:
    ___ reduced tension   ___ happier   ___ satisfied
    ___ other (specify) _____

3. a. Have you ever experienced a runner's high?

    b. If "Yes" to question 3a, describe what it felt like and under what environmental conditions (e.g., weather) it occurred.

    c. If "Yes" to question 3a, how long did you run?

    d. If "Yes" to question 3a, how often have you experienced a runner's high?

4. a. Have you ever know anyone who has been addicted to exercise?

    b. If "Yes" to question 4a, was this person positively or negatively addicted?
    Positively   Negatively

    c. If "Yes" to question 4a, how could you tell this person was addicted?

Activity 17.2	# Exercise and Psychological Well-Being Match Test

Do this activity after reading chapter 17 of *Foundations of Sport and Exercise Psychology.*

Directions: Match the proper term or phrase with the most appropriate response or definition. Use each term only once, although not all terms will be used.

a. anaerobic exercise   e. aerobic exercise   i. acute effects

b. chronic effects   f. neurotransmitters   j. time-out or distraction

c. runner's high   g. negative addiction   k. mood

d. positive addiction   h. self-esteem   l. self-concept

___ 1. This condition is characterized by a dependence on exercise and severe depression when one is not able to engage in exercise.

___ 2. A physiological explanation for how exercise enhances psychological well-being.

___ 3. The long-term effects of exercise.

___ 4. Physical activity that increases the activity of the pulmonary and cardiovascular systems (during which the body uses and transports oxygen to the working muscles to maintain activity).

___ 5. Short-duration exercise of insufficient intensity to require much transportation of oxygen to the working muscles.

___ 6. A psychological explanation for how exercise enhances psychological well-being.

___ 7. A euphoric sensation, usually unexpected, of heightened well-being, an enhanced appreciation of nature, and the transcendence of time and space.

___ 8. A state of emotional or affective arousal of varying degrees of an impermanent nature.

___ 9. This all-encompassing term focuses on how we feel about ourselves and our capabilities.

___10. The short-term effects of exercise.

Justifying Exercise and Psychological Well-Being

Activity 17.3

Do this activity after reading chapter 17 of *Foundations of Sport and Exercise Psychology.*

Directions: Respond to the following scenario.

You have applied for a position as the fitness director for the local YMCA. On a job interview a member of the search committee states that they all have a pretty good understanding of the physical benefits of exercise, but not the psychological benefits. Respond to the following questions of this individual.

1. What if, any, benefits does exercise have on psychological well-being?

2. What specific types of exercise does one need to do to ensure any psychological benefits?

3. Are there any negative psychological drawbacks to exercising regularly?

Answers to Selected Chapter 17 Activities

Activity 17.2: Exercise and Psychological Well-Being Match Test

1. g
2. f
3. b

4. e
5. a
6. j
7. c
8. k
9. l
10. i

18

Exercise Behavior and Adherence

concepts

- People indicate that they exercise in an effort to achieve weight control, reduce risk of cardiovascular disease, reduce stress and depression, enhance self-esteem, and increase enjoyment. The major reasons why people drop out include a perceived lack of time, lack of energy, and a lack of motivation. Both the psychological and physical benefits of exercising can be cited to help persuade sedentary people to initiate an exercise program.

- One of the most frequently used models of understanding the process of exercise adoption and adherence is the transtheoretical model. This model proposes that individuals move through five stages of exercise adoption that include: precontemplation; contemplation; preparation; action; and maintenance. The key practical implication is to match the exercise intervention to the stage a person is in.

- Personal determinants of exercise behavior include demographic variables (e.g., gender, socioeconomic status); cognitive and personality variables (e.g., self-efficacy, knowledge of health and exercise); and behaviors (e.g., smoking, diet). Environmental factors include the social environment (e.g., social support, past family influences); the physical environment (e.g., access to facilities, weather); and the characteristics of the physical activity (e.g., intensity, group or individual program).

- To increase exercise adherence one can use five approaches: (1) environmental (e.g., prompts, contracting); (2) reinforcement (e.g., rewards for attendance, feedback); (3) goal-setting and cognition (e.g., association or dissociation); (4) decision-making (e.g., decision balance sheet); and (5) social support (e.g., classmates, family).

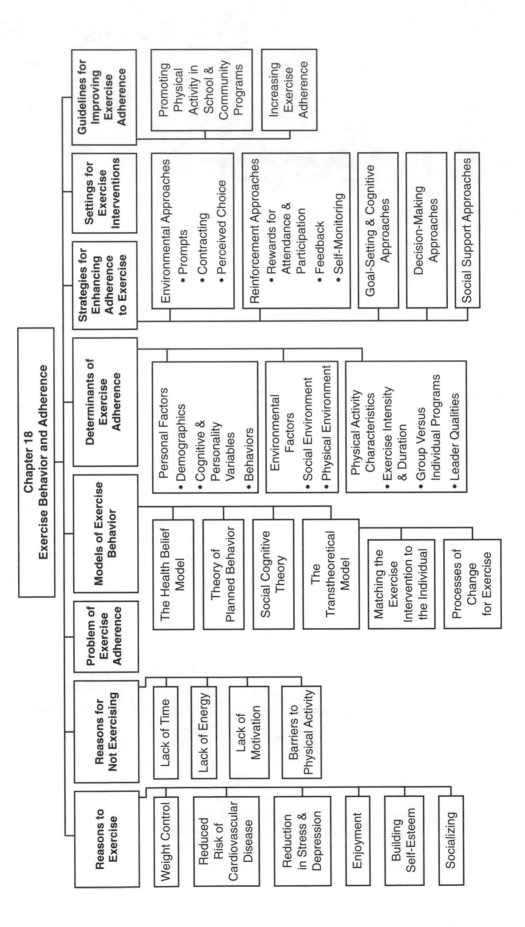

Chapter 18
Exercise Behavior and Adherence

Reasons to Exercise
- Weight Control
- Reduced Risk of Cardiovascular Disease
- Reduction in Stress & Depression
- Enjoyment
- Building Self-Esteem
- Socializing

Reasons for Not Exercising
- Lack of Time
- Lack of Energy
- Lack of Motivation
- Barriers to Physical Activity

Problem of Exercise Adherence

Models of Exercise Behavior
- The Health Belief Model
- Theory of Planned Behavior
- Social Cognitive Theory
- The Transtheoretical Model
- Matching the Exercise Intervention to the Individual
- Processes of Change for Exercise

Determinants of Exercise Adherence
- Personal Factors
  - Demographics
  - Cognitive & Personality Variables
  - Behaviors
- Environmental Factors
  - Social Environment
  - Physical Environment
- Physical Activity Characteristics
  - Exercise Intensity & Duration
  - Group Versus Individual Programs
  - Leader Qualities

Strategies for Enhancing Adherence to Exercise
- Environmental Approaches
  - Prompts
  - Contracting
  - Perceived Choice
- Reinforcement Approaches
  - Rewards for Attendance & Participation
  - Feedback
  - Self-Monitoring
- Goal-Setting & Cognitive Approaches
- Decision-Making Approaches
- Social Support Approaches

Settings for Exercise Interventions

Guidelines for Improving Exercise Adherence
- Promoting Physical Activity in School & Community Programs
- Increasing Exercise Adherence

• To maximize participation adherence, exercise leaders should make the exercise enjoyable and convenient, provide social support, encourage exercising with a friend, provide rewards for attendance and participation, and offer participants a range of activities from which to choose.

Activity 18.1

Do this activity after reading chapter 18 of *Foundations of Sport and Exercise Psychology.*

Why Do I Exercise?

Directions: Consider your own exercise experiences and habits and respond to the following questions.

1. Identify the reasons you exercise or have exercised in the past.

2. Now think of the reasons you have used for not exercising or stopping exercise in the past. List the most prevalent reasons for you.

Now compare your answers to questions 1 and 2 to the reasons for exercising, not exercising, and stopping exercise on pages 372 to 376 of *Foundations of Sport and Exercise Psychology.* Were your responses similar? In what ways were they different?

Activity 18.2

Do this activity after reading chapter 18 of *Foundations of Sport and Exercise Psychology.*

Matching Exercise Interventions to Individuals in Varying Stages of Behavioral Change

Directions: The five stages of change in the transtheoretical model are discussed in your textbook (pages 377-378). Moreover, the key practical implication derived from this theory is that exercise interventions must be matched to an individual's stage of behavioral change. Indicate what you would do to motivate and encourage desirable exercise behavior participation for a person in each of the following stages of behavioral change.

1. Precontemplation "Couch Potato" Stage:

2. Contemplation "Thought of Getting Off the Couch" Stage:

3. Preparation "Exercising Some" Stage:

4. Action "Risk of Relapse" Stage:

5. Maintenance "Regular Exerciser" Stage:

Activity 18.3   # Should I Exercise?—A Decision Balance Sheet

Do this activity after reading chapter 18 of *Foundations of Sport and Exercise Psychology*.

Directions: Contact someone you know who does not exercise regularly. Work with him or her to complete the decision balance sheet below.

Gains to self
(e.g., better health)

1.
2.
3.
4.
5.

Losses to self
(e.g., less time with family)

1.
2.
3.
4.
5.

Gains to important others
(e.g., become more attractive to others)

1.
2.
3.
4.
5.

Losses to important others
(e.g., less time to study, get good grades, and please my parents)

1.
2.
3.
4.
5.

Approval from others
(e.g., my folks would like me to)

1.
2.
3.
4.
5.

Disapproval from others
(e.g., my friends would think I am wasting my time)

1.
2.
3.
4.
5.

Self-approval
(e.g., feel better about myself)

1.
2.
3.
4.
5.

Self-disapproval
(e.g., look foolish in exercise clothes)

1.
2.
3.
4
5.

Activity 18.4

Do this activity after reading chapter 18 of *Foundations of Sport and Exercise Psychology.*

Enhancing Exercise Adherence

Directions: Your university has recently opened a multimillion dollar recreation facility. Administrators are alarmed at the number of students who are not engaged in regular exercise programs. As an exercise and sport psychology expert, you have been hired by the Student Government to devise strategies to enhance adherence. Indicate what you would consider and do in each area.

1. Personal factors:

2. Physical factors:

3. Situational factors:

4. Behavioral factors:

5. Programmatic factors:

Answers to Selected Chapter 18 Activities

Activity 18.2: Matching Exercise Interventions to Individuals in Varying Stages of Behavioral Change

1. Inform the person of the benefits and barriers to physical activity; provide suggestions for leading an increasingly active lifestyle (e.g., take the stairs instead of the elevator, walk to nearby store instead of driving, take dog on increasingly longer walks every day).

2. Help the participant be more physically active for 30 minutes a day, three to five times a week (take dog on increasingly longer walks every day); set short-term goals, apply time management skills, and self-rewards for activities.

3. Set short-term goals, apply time management skills (e.g., set regular time for exercise), and self-rewards for activities.

4. Troubleshoot factors that could make exercisers relapse into nonexercise modes (e.g., illness, check boredom levels); cross train to offset boredom; make sure social support is provided (e.g., exercise with a buddy).

5. Cross train to offset boredom; make sure social support is provided.

Activity 18.4:   Enhancing Exercise Adherence

1. To help students feel more confident (or efficacious) about getting started in an exercise program I would implement the following: (a) tours of the recreation center the first week of each semester; (b) introductory exercise classes during the first week of each semester; and (c) free instruction on how to use all equipment in the recreation center.

2. Since one of the main rationalizations for not exercising is a lack of time, I will schedule exercise classes during the lunch hour and in the evenings when most students do not have classes. Additionally, I will set up on-campus shuttles from dorms to the recreation center at night so students can get to and from the rec center safely.

3. To increase social support I will implement a "fitness friends" program where students can sign up to have an exercise buddy.

4. Students who have had early experiences in sport and exercise are more likely to be current participants in physical activity. Through the recreation center, I will set up a program to encourage current exercisers to bring a friend (who is not currently exercising) to the rec center for a "fun" day. This "fun" day will include tours and basic exercise or sport instruction.

5. Because of the wide variety of fitness levels and interests of the students, different types of exercise and intensity levels will be provided. Also, although exercise adherence is facilitated by group exercise, some students may prefer to exercise alone. To help those students, the rec center will teach students how to start an exercise program and how to monitor their progress.

Athletic Injuries and Psychology

concepts

- Psychological factors influence the incidence of injury, responses to injury, and injury recovery.

- Psychological antecedents of injury include major life stress attitudes such as "act tough and give 110%" and "if you're injured, you're worthless."

- Athletes must learn to distinguish between the normal discomfort of training and the pain of injury. They should understand that a "no pain, no gain" attitude can predispose them to injury.

- Injured athletes and exercisers exhibit various psychological reactions, including injury-relevant information processing; emotional upheaval and reactive behavior; and positive outlook and coping.

- Warning signs of poor adjustment to injury include feelings of anger and confusion; obsession with the question of when one can return to play; denial (e.g., "the injury is no big deal"); repeatedly coming back too soon and experiencing reinjury; exaggerated bragging about accomplishments; dwelling on minor physical complaints; guilt about letting the team down; withdrawal from significant others; rapid mood swings; and statements indicating that no matter what is done, recovery will not occur.

- Psychological foundations of injury rehabilitation include building rapport with the injured individual; educating him or her about the nature of the injury and the injury-recovery process; teaching specific psychological coping skills, such as goal-setting, relaxation techniques, and imagery; preparing him or her to cope with setbacks in rehabilitation; and fostering social support.

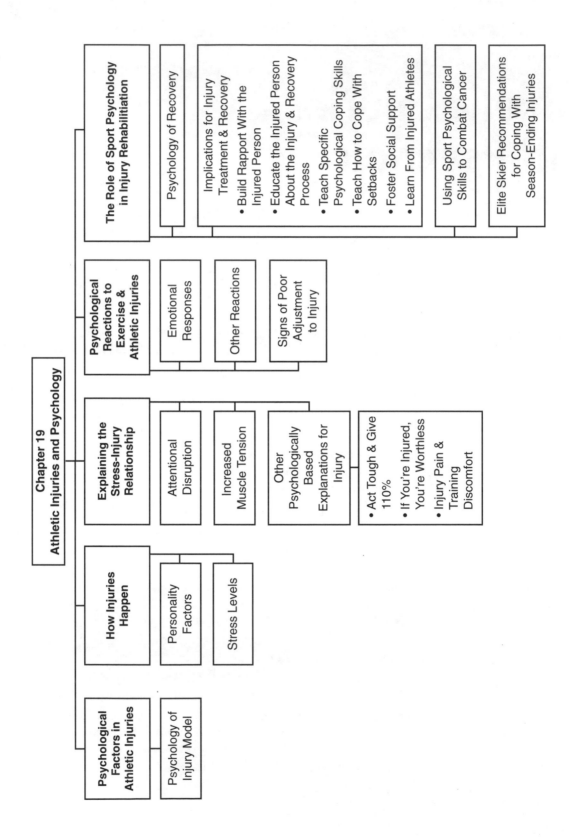

Chapter 19
Athletic Injuries and Psychology

Psychological Factors in Athletic Injuries

- Psychology of Injury Model

How Injuries Happen

- Personality Factors
- Stress Levels

Explaining the Stress-Injury Relationship

- Attentional Disruption
- Increased Muscle Tension
- Other Psychologically Based Explanations for Injury
  - Act Tough & Give 110%
  - If You're Injured, You're Worthless
  - Injury Pain & Training Discomfort

Psychological Reactions to Exercise & Athletic Injuries

- Emotional Responses
- Other Reactions
- Signs of Poor Adjustment to Injury

The Role of Sport Psychology in Injury Rehabilitiation

- Psychology of Recovery
- Implications for Injury Treatment & Recovery
  - Build Rapport With the Injured Person
  - Educate the Injured Person About the Injury & Recovery Process
  - Teach Specific Psychological Coping Skills
  - Teach How to Cope With Setbacks
  - Foster Social Support
  - Learn From Injured Athletes
- Using Sport Psychological Skills to Combat Cancer
- Elite Skier Recommendations for Coping With Season-Ending Injuries

Activity 19.1

Understanding the Stress-Injury Relationship

Do this activity after reading pages 397 to 403 of *Foundations of Sport and Exercise Psychology.*

Directions: After reading the "Explaining the Stress-Injury Relationship" section of the text (pages 401–403) respond to the following questions.

1. Explain how stress can cause injury as a result of attentional disruptions; provide examples.

2. What role does increased muscle tension play in the stress-injury relationship?

3. What psychological attitudes predispose athletes and exercisers to injury?

Activity 19.2

Psychology of Athletic Injury Class Discussions/Interviews

Do this activity after reading chapter 19 of *Foundations of Sport and Exercise Psychology.*

Directions: This exercise increases your awareness of the role that psychological factors play in injury occurrence and recovery. Your instructor will ask volunteers to share their injury experiences with the class, or you should identify an individual you know who has experienced a major athletic or exercise injury and interview him or her. Take notes on what the speakers or athlete interviewed says and ask follow-up questions where appropriate.

1. What was the nature and extent of your injury?

2. How did your injury occur?

3. What did you feel like when
   a. you were injured?

   b. you learned about the severity of your injury?

   c. one week after the injury?

   d. one month after the injury?

4. What was your injury rehabilitation process like?

    a. Did you experience any barriers to recovery?

    b. What factors facilitated your recovery?

5. Did you fully recover from your injury?

    a. If so, what was it like resuming normal physical activity?

    b. If not, how do you continue to cope with your injury?

 Activity 19.3

Designing a Sport Psychology Injury Rehabilitation Program

Do this activity after reading chapter 19 of *Foundations of Sport and Exercise Psychology.*

Directions: Your friend, who is an athletic trainer, learns that you have taken a sport and exercise psychology class that includes a section on psychological factors in athletic injuries and asks you to talk to the student trainers about designing psychologically based rehabilitation programs for injured athletes. Describe the major topics and supporting information that you would include in your presentation.

Answers to Selected Chapter 19 Activities

Activity 19.1:   Understanding the Stress-Injury Relationship

1. It has been found that stress disrupts an athlete's attention by reducing peripheral attention (e.g., a stressed quarterback does not see a defender rushing from the offside because his attentional field is narrowed) and causing distracting and irrelevant thoughts (e.g., a jogger steps in a hole because she is preoccupied with worry during her run).

2. Stress often leads to increased muscle tension, which interferes with normal coordination and increases the chances of injury.

3. Act tough and give 110%; if you are injured, you are worthless.

Activity 19.3: Designing a Sport Psychology Injury Rehabilitation Program

1. Explain typical psychological reactions to injury (e.g., injury-relevant information processing, emotional upheaval and reactive behavior, positive outlook and coping) and other emotional responses (identity loss, fear and anxiety, lack of confidence, performance decrements).

2. Warning signs of poor adjustment to injury (See page 405 in *Foundations of Sport and Exercise Psychology.*)

3. Strategies for assisting injured athletes recovery:
   - Build rapport with the injured person.
   - Educate the injured person about the injury-recovery process.
   - Teach specific psychological skills (e.g., goal-setting, positive self-talk, imagery and relaxation training).
   - Teach athletes how to cope with setbacks.
   - Foster social support.
   - Learn from injured athletes.
   - Have athletes talk to and learn from other or formerly injured athletes.

Addictive and Unhealthy Behaviors

concepts

- Anorexia nervosa and bulimia are the two most common eating disorders. Anorexia is characterized by an intense sense of gaining weight and a distorted body image, whereas bulimia is characterized by recurrent episodes of binge eating and regular, self-induced vomiting. Athletes in sports where weight is a concern (such as wrestling, gymnastics, and track) appear to have higher rates of eating-related problems than does the general population.

- The signs and symptoms of bulimia and anorexia nervosa are both physical (e.g., weight too low, bloating, swollen salivary glands) and psychological/behavioral (excessive dieting, binge eating, preoccupation with food). People with these disorders need specialized assistance. Fitness professionals must be able to recognize the physical and psychological signs of eating disorders and refer people that show such symptoms for specialized help.

- Substance abuse is one of the most severe problems facing our society. Although it is difficult to get exact figures regarding the use of certain drugs, we do know that many athletes and exercisers take both performance enhancing drugs and recreational drugs, and both types of drugs have dangerous side effects.

- Athletes and exercisers usually take drugs for reasons that are physical (e.g., to enhance performance), psychological (e.g., to relieve stress), or social (e.g., to satisfy peer pressure). Sports and exercise professionals can help prevent substance abuse by setting a good example, educating participants, and providing a supportive environment that addresses the reasons individuals take drugs.

- Gambling is often not thought of as a serious problem, but, in fact, like the abuse of drugs and alcohol, it can be an addiction. Compulsive gamblers are usually boastful, arrogant, have unbounded optimism, and are extremely competitive.

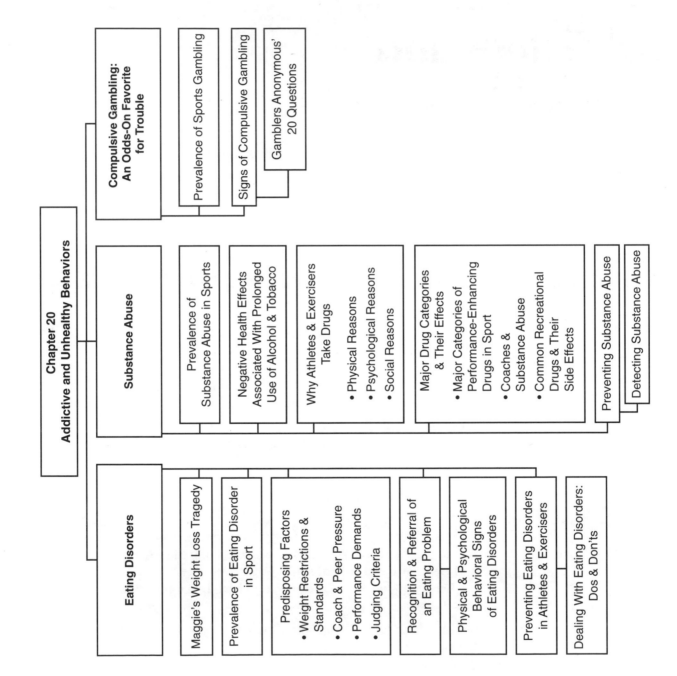

Chapter 20
Addictive and Unhealthy Behaviors

Eating Disorders

Maggie's Weight Loss Tragedy

Prevalence of Eating Disorder in Sport

Predisposing Factors
- Weight Restrictions & Standards
- Coach & Peer Pressure
- Performance Demands
- Judging Criteria

Recognition & Referral of an Eating Problem

Physical & Psychological Behavioral Signs of Eating Disorders

Preventing Eating Disorders in Athletes & Exercisers

Dealing With Eating Disorders: Dos & Don'ts

Substance Abuse

Prevalence of Substance Abuse in Sports

Negative Health Effects Associated With Prolonged Use of Alcohol & Tobacco

Why Athletes & Exercisers Take Drugs
- Physical Reasons
- Psychological Reasons
- Social Reasons

Major Drug Categories & Their Effects
- Major Categories of Performance-Enhancing Drugs in Sport
- Coaches & Substance Abuse
- Common Recreational Drugs & Their Side Effects

Preventing Substance Abuse

Detecting Substance Abuse

Compulsive Gambling: An Odds-On Favorite for Trouble

Prevalence of Sports Gambling

Signs of Compulsive Gambling

Gamblers Anonymous' 20 Questions

> **Activity 20.1**

Do this activity after reading chapter 20 of *Foundations of Sport and Exercise Psychology*.

Eating Disorder Confrontation

Directions: This is a role-playing exercise. Work in pairs (with someone of your choosing if you do not do this exercise in class). One person assumes the role of someone with an eating disorder; the other plays the role of an exercise and sport science professional who confronts the abuser and asks if he or she has an eating problem. After completing the role-play, rate the confronter using the following checklist.

Eating Disorder Confrontation Checklist

1. Was supportive and empathetic	Yes	No
2. Expressed concern about general feelings, not weight specifically	Yes	No
3. Emphasized the importance of good nutrition	Yes	No
4. Made referrals to a specific person	Yes	No
5. Made an appointment with a specialist for the person	Yes	No
6. Did not demand the problem be stopped immediately	Yes	No
7. Did not ask the person to leave team or curtail participation	Yes	No
8. Did not recommend weight loss or gain	Yes	No

> **Activity 20.2**

Do this activity after reading chapter 20 of *Foundations of Sport and Exercise Psychology*.

Signs and Symptoms of Substance Abuse

Directions: Working in small groups identify as many signs and symptoms of substance abuse as you can.

> **Activity 20.3**

Do this activity after reading chapter 20 of *Foundations of Sport and Exercise Psychology*.

Gambling on Your Campus

Directions: In the text it was indicated that considerable gambling takes place on high school and college campuses. For this exercise your job is to determine if this is the case. Working by yourself or with several students from class, interview students who were or are highly involved in sports. Ask them the following questions. Make sure that their responses are kept confidential, and let them know this before they begin.

1. Do you know if many students gamble on sports?

2. Have you ever met anyone who gambled on sports?

3. Have you ever gambled on sports?

4. If "Yes" to questions 1, 2 or 3, what sports were the focus of the gambling and how much was bet?

5. What do you or they enjoy about sports gambling?

6. What, if any, are the disadvantages of sports betting?

7. What would you do to help a friend that you suspect is heavily involved in sports gambling?

Note: Examine your responses relative to the section on sports gambling in chapter 20, pages 427 to 429. What did you learn? Did anything surprise you?

Answers to Selected Chapter 20 Activities

Activity 20.2:   Signs and Symptoms of Substance Abuse

- Changes in behavior (lack of motivation, tardiness, absenteeism)
- Changes in peer group
- Major changes in personality
- Major changes in athletic or academic performance
- Apathetic or listless behaviors
- Impaired judgement
- Poor coordination
- Poor hygiene and grooming
- Profuse sweating
- Muscular twitches or tremors

Burnout and Overtraining

concepts

- Overtraining is the abnormal extension of the training process with loads too intense for athletes to adapt to. Staleness is the end result of overtraining, a state in which athletes have difficulty maintaining their standard training regimens and performance results. Burnout is a more exhaustive psychophysiological response of withdrawal from excessive training and competition demands.

- Three sport-specific models of burnout include: (1) the cognitive-affective stress model that presents a four-stage process of burnout involving situational demands, cognitive appraisal of the situation, physiological responses, and coping behaviors; (2) the negative training stress model focuses more attention on responses to physical training, although psychological factors are also seen as important; and (3) the unidimensional identity development and external control model is more sociological in nature, viewing stress as a symptom of social and societal factors.

- Successful athletes exhibit high levels of vigor and low levels of negative mood states, an optimal combination. Overtrained athletes show an inverted iceberg profile, with negative states pronounced.

- Causes of burnout and overtraining include physical concerns (e.g., injury, high frequency and intensity of training); logistical concerns (e.g., travel grind, time demands); social-interpersonal concerns (e.g., dissatisfaction with social life, negative parental influences); and psychological concerns (e.g., inappropriate expectations, lack of enjoyment).

- Common symptoms of overtraining include apathy, mood changes, muscle pain, and appetite loss, whereas common symptoms of burnout include a lack of caring, emotional isolation, and increased anxiety.

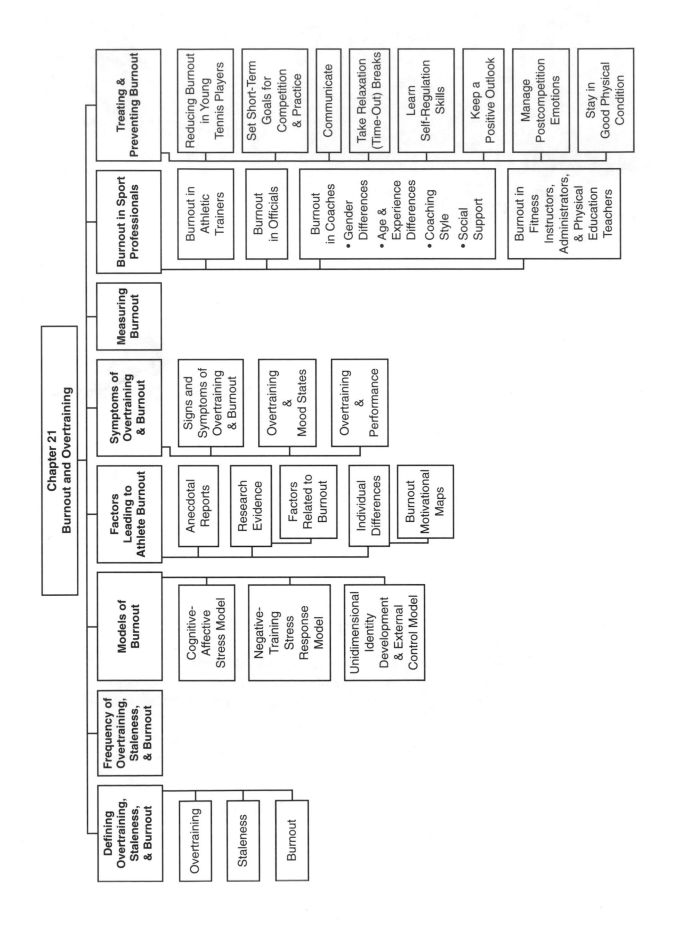

Chapter 21
Burnout and Overtraining

Defining Overtraining, Staleness, & Burnout
- Overtraining
- Staleness
- Burnout

Frequency of Overtraining, Staleness, & Burnout

Models of Burnout
- Cognitive-Affective Stress Model
- Negative-Training Stress Response Model
- Unidimensional Identity Development & External Control Model

Factors Leading to Athlete Burnout
- Anecdotal Reports
- Research Evidence
- Factors Related to Burnout
- Individual Differences
- Burnout Motivational Maps

Symptoms of Overtraining & Burnout
- Signs and Symptoms of Overtraining & Burnout
- Overtraining & Mood States
- Overtraining & Performance

Measuring Burnout

Burnout in Sport Professionals
- Burnout in Athletic Trainers
- Burnout in Officials
- Burnout in Coaches
  - Gender Differences
  - Age & Experience Differences
  - Coaching Style
  - Social Support
- Burnout in Fitness Instructors, Administrators, & Physical Education Teachers

Treating & Preventing Burnout
- Reducing Burnout in Young Tennis Players
- Set Short-Term Goals for Competition & Practice
- Communicate
- Take Relaxation (Time-Out) Breaks
- Learn Self-Regulation Skills
- Keep a Positive Outlook
- Manage Postcompetition Emotions
- Stay in Good Physical Condition

- To prevent or reduce the probability of burnout in sport, set short-term goals for practice and competitions, take relaxation breaks, keep a positive outlook, and learn self-regulation.

Differentiating Between Overtraining, Staleness, and Burnout

Do this activity after reading pages 434 to 436 of *Foundations of Sport and Exercise Psychology.*

Directions: Answer the following questions.

1. What is overtraining?

2. What is staleness?

3. What is burnout?

4. What is the relationship between overtraining, staleness, and burnout?

Factors Related to Athlete Burnout

Do this activity after reading chapter 21 of *Foundations of Sport and Exercise Psychology.*

Directions: If you have an athletic background, think of the point in the season that you were most tired, stressed, and least motivated. (If you do not have an athletic background, find an athlete to interview.) On the table (next page) circle the specific situational demands, cognitive appraisal of the situation factors, psychophysiological responses, behavioral responses, and personality and motivational factors that characterized your (or the athlete's) situation.

Factors Related to Athlete Burnout

Situational demands	Cognitive appraisal of the situation	Physiological/ Psychological responses	Behavioral responses	Personality and motivational factors
High conflicting demands	Perceived overload	Decreased motivation	Physical withdrawal	High trait anxiety
Lack of control/powerlessness; dependency	Few meaningful accomplishments	Fatigue	Emotional withdrawal	Low self-esteem and low perceived competence
High expectations by self and others	Lack of meaning and devaluation of activity	Decreased concentration	Psychological withdrawal	Competitive orientations: fear of failure, fear of poor evaluation
Low social support	Lack of enjoyment	Weight gain or loss	Decreased performance	Unidimensional self-concept
Excessive demands on time	Chronic stress	Illness or injury susceptibility	Giving up during play, tanking	High need to please others
Limited social relationships	Learned helplessness	Moodiness and impatience	Rigid, inappropriate behavior	Low assertiveness
Parental involvement: restrictive, inconsistent feedback, negative feedback	Decreased life satisfaction	Poor sleep	Interpersonal difficulties	Self-critical
Coach involvement: inconsistent feedback, negative feedback	Identity crisis	Anger; irritability	Lowered school performance	Perfectionism
Injuries	Stifled; trapped	Muscle soreness		Low perceived control
Training loads: repetitive, high volume, number of competitions		Boredom		Low frustration

Adapted from Gould et al., 1996.

Signs and Symptoms of Overtraining and Burnout Panel

Activity 21.3

Do this activity after reading chapter 21 of *Foundations of Sport and Exercise Psychology.*

Directions: Your instructor will form a panel of athletes from your class, or you may interview an athlete or former athlete whom you know. Ask the panel (athlete) the following questions about overtraining and burnout. Feel free to add your own questions.

1. When did you burn out?

2. In what sport or physical activity were you participating?

3. How intensely were you training when you burned out?

4. How did you feel physically at this time?

5. How did you feel psychologically at this time?

6. Relative to questions 4 and 5, for how long did you feel this way?

7. Did your symptoms occur suddenly or build up over time?

Activity 21.4

Treating and Preventing Burnout

Do this activity after reading chapter 21 of *Foundations of Sport and Exercise Psychology.*

Directions: In small groups (or by yourself), discuss how burnout can be treated or prevented by employing each of the following general strategies.

1. Goal-setting:

2. Communication:

3. Breaks and time-outs:

4. Self-regulation skills:

5. Positive focusing/orientation:

6. Postcompetition emotion management:

7. Good physical conditioning:

Answers to Selected Chapter 21 Activities

Activity 21.1:   Differentiating Between Overtraining, Staleness, and Burnout

1. An abnormal extension of the training process of purposefully overloading an athlete or exerciser, but instead of resulting in positive adaptations, the extension of the process without adequate rest culminates in staleness.

2. A physiological state of overtraining that manifests as deteriorated athletic readiness. A stale athlete has difficulty maintaining standard training regimens and can no longer achieve previous performance results.

3. An exhaustive psychophysiological response exhibited as a result of frequent, sometimes extreme, and generally ineffective efforts to meet excessive training and competitive demands. It involves a psychological, emotional, and sometimes physical withdrawal from a formerly enjoyable activity in response to excessive stress.

4. Overtraining can lead to staleness, and further training or demands over time can lead to burnout.

Facilitating Psychological Growth and Development

22

Children's Psychological Development Through Sport

concepts

- The youth sport experience can have important lifelong effects on the personality and psychological development of children. However, adult leadership is crucial to assure a beneficial experience.

- Children cite many reasons for sport participation, including having fun, skill improvement, and being with friends. They also have various reasons for dropping out of sport, including new or additional interests in other activities. Underlying these motives is the young athlete's need to feel worthy and competent.

- Peer relationships in youth sport affect a child's sense of acceptance, level of motivation, and self-esteem. Adult leaders should provide time for children to be with friends and make new friends, encourage positive peer reinforcement, emphasize teamwork and the pursuit of group goals, and teach children to respect others and refrain from verbal aggression.

- Most young athletes do not experience excessive levels of competitive stress in sport, but a significant minority do. Moreover, a profile of the personal characteristics and situations that lead to heightened stress in children exists.

- Stress-induced burnout is a specialized sport withdrawal in which young athletes discontinue or curtail involvement in response to long-term stress.

- Research findings in sport psychology have clearly shown that certain coaching behaviors are associated with positive psychological development in children. Effective coaching behaviors include having realistic expectations; using techniques that provide youngsters with positive, encouraging, and sincere feedback; rewarding effort and correct technique as much as outcomes; modifying skill requirements and rules; and employing a positive approach to error correction.

Chapter 22
Children's Psychological Development Through Sport

Why a Psychology of the Young Athlete?

Why Children Participate in Sports
- Motives for Youth Sport Participation

Why Children Discontinue Participation in Sports
- Perceived Competence
- Sport-Specific Versus Sport-General Dropouts
- Youth Sport Participation: Implications for Practice
- Strategies for Structuring Sport Situations to Meet the Needs of Young Athletes

The Role of Friends in Youth Sport
- Peer Relationships & Children's Psychological Development
- Friendship in Sport: Implications for Practice

Stress & Burnout in Children's Competitive Sport
- Are Young Athletes Under Too Much Stress?
- Factors Associated With Heightened State Anxiety in Young Athletes
- Situational Sources of Stress
- Stress-Induced Burnout
- Factors Associated With Burnout in Young Athletes
- Dealing With Stressed Children: Implications for Practice

Effective Coaching Practices for Young Athletes
- What Research Says About Coaching Children
- Coaching Young Athletes: Implications for Practice

The Role of Parents
- Parenting Research in Youth Sports
- Educating Parents
- Sport Parent Responsibilities & Code of Conduct
- Understanding the Tricky Business of Parental Support

- Parental attitudes and behaviors have major effects, both positive and negative, on young athletes' sport involvement, motivation, self-esteem, and mental health. Educating parents and maintaining open lines of coach-parent communication are important ways to ensure beneficial parental influence in children's sport.

Motives for Discontinuing Youth Sports/ Sources of Stress in Young Athletes

Activity 22.1

Do this activity after reading chapter 22 of *Foundations of Sport and Exercise Psychology*.

Directions: Pose the following questions about *youth sports* motivation and sources of stress to the panel organized by your instructor, or answer them yourself based on your own youth sports experience. Feel free to add your own questions on these topics.

Background:

1. What sport do (did) you play? When and for how long?

Motivation:

1. What were your motives for participation?

2. When and under what conditions did you discontinue involvement?

3. Why did you discontinue?

4. Did you ever play the sport again?

5. Do (did) you play other sports?

Sources of stress:

1. Was youth sports participation ever stressful for you?

2. If so, when did you become stressed?

3. If so, what were the causes of your stress?

4. How did you handle your stress?

5. How did the stress of youth sport participation compare to other activities you were involved in (school test, drama, band)?

| Activity 22.2 |

Spaghetti Toes Relaxation

Do this activity after reading chapter 22 of *Foundations of Sport and Exercise Psychology*.

Directions: You can do this exercise in one of two ways. If you are able to work with a child between 8 and 10 years of age, lead the child through a relaxation training session following the spaghetti toes directions shown in the box on page 466 of *Foundations of Sport and Exercise Psychology*. Then ask the child the following questions. If you do not have access to a young child, tape-record the spaghetti toes directions on page 466 and then play the tape to yourself as your relax. Following the relaxation session answer the questions below.

1. What did your body feel like at the start of our spaghetti toes activity? How about when you were at the end?

2. Did you like the way you felt?

3. Would you want to do this game again? Why? Why not?

Activity 22.3

Educating Youth Sport Parents

Do this activity after reading chapter 22 of *Foundations of Sport and Exercise Psychology.*

Directions: You are coaching a youth basketball team made up of fifteen children ages 10 to 11. Last year the league struggled with numerous problems caused by over-involved parents who yelled at coaches, argued with officials, and interfered with games. One of the ways the league hopes to rectify this state of affairs is to have all coaches schedule a youth basketball parent orientation meeting prior to the start of the season. List what you would cover in such a meeting with the parents of your team.

Answers to Selected Chapter 22 Activities

Activity 22.3: Educating Youth Sport Parents

1. My qualifications as a coach.

2. My philosophy of coaching.

3. The roles played by athletes, coaches, and parents (see sport parent responsibilities and code of conduct on page 470 in *Foundations of Sport and Exercise Psychology*).

4. Sportspersonship.

5. Team rules.

Aggression in Sport

concepts

- Aggression is behavior directed toward the goal of harming or injuring another living being. For an act to be considered aggression it must meet four criteria: it must be an actual behavior; involve harm or injury; be directed toward another living thing; and involve intent. Aggression is distinct from assertive behavior in sport.

- Strong support has been found for the revised frustration-aggression and social learning theories of aggression. Frustration predisposes individuals to aggressiveness, and aggression occurs if it has been learned to be an appropriate reaction to frustration. Modeling and reinforcement can be powerful determinants of aggressive behavior.

- There is little support for the instinct theory of aggression or its tangential notion of catharsis (the idea that aggression is blown off through socially acceptable ways).

- An inconsistent relationship has been found between aggression and performance; in some cases aggression is associated with enhanced performance and in other cases it is not.

- Implications for helping sport participants control aggression include: recognizing when aggression is most likely to occur; teaching athletes how to handle potentially aggressive situations; teaching appropriate behavior; and modifying inappropriate actions.

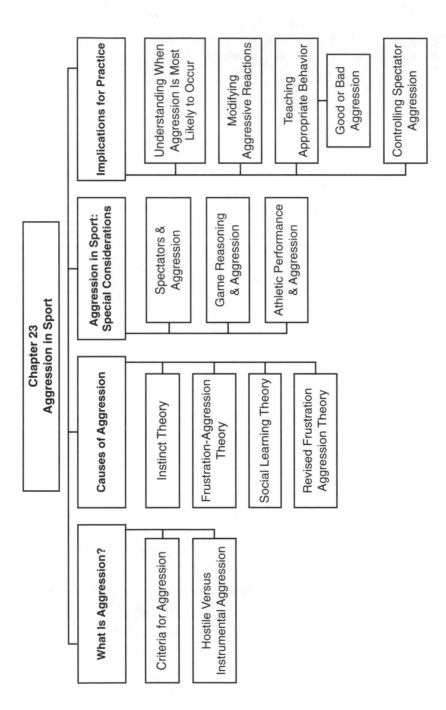

**Chapter 23
Aggression in Sport**

What Is Aggression?

Criteria for Aggression

Hostile Versus Instrumental Aggression

Causes of Aggression

Instinct Theory

Frustration-Aggression Theory

Social Learning Theory

Revised Frustration Aggression Theory

Aggression in Sport: Special Considerations

Spectators & Aggression

Game Reasoning & Aggression

Athletic Performance & Aggression

Implications for Practice

Understanding When Aggression Is Most Likely to Occur

Modifying Aggressive Reactions

Teaching Appropriate Behavior

Good or Bad Aggression

Controlling Spectator Aggression

Activity 23.1

Defining Aggression

Do this activity after reading chapter 23 of *Foundations of Sport and Exercise Psychology*.

Directions: Gill (1986) has identified four criteria to use in judging whether aggression occurs. These include:

1. Being a behavior
2. Involving harm or injury
3. Being directed toward a living thing
4. Involving intent

Using Gill's four criteria, indicate whether you consider the behavior in each of these situations to be aggressive (A) or nonaggressive (N) by circling the appropriate letter.

1. A football safety delivers an extremely vicious but *legal* hit to a wide receiver and later indicates he wanted to punish the receiver and make him think twice about coming across the middle.   A   N

2. A football safety delivers an extremely vicious and *illegal* hit to a wide receiver but had no intention of punishing him.   A   N

3. A basketball coach breaks a chair in protesting a disputed call.   A   N

4. Marcia, a field hockey midfielder, uses her stick to purposefully hit her opponent in the shin in retaliation for her opponent's doing the same thing to her.   A   N

5. A race car driver kills a fellow competitor by running into the competitor's stalled car coming out of a turn.   A   N

6. Trying to make an opposing field goal kicker worry and think about the negative ramifications of a game-winning field goal, Coach Sullivan calls a time-out.   A   N

7. Barry knows that John is very sensitive and self-conscious about his ability to putt under pressure, so he tells John that Coach Hall said if he does not putt better he will be replaced in the lineup. Coach Hall never said this.   A   N

8. Jane beans Fran with a fastball that got away from her.   A   N

Recognizing When Aggression Is Most Likely to Occur

Activity 23.2

Do this activity after reading chapter 23 of *Foundations of Sport and Exercise Psychology*.

Directions: Working alone or with a small group of classmates, discuss the following questions about when aggression is most likely to occur.

1. What sport situations are most frustrating and arousing for participants?

2. In frustrating sport situations, why do people sometimes act aggressively and other times not act aggressively?

3. What socially learned cues in sport signal the appropriateness of being aggressive?

Activity 23.3

Controlling Spectator Aggression

Do this activity after reading chapter 23 of *Foundations of Sport and Exercise Psychology.*

Directions: You are a member of the Athletic Advisory Board of a high school in your community. Unfortunately, recent basketball and football games have been plagued by spectator violence often ignited after on-court altercations. Indicate what actions you would recommend that the Athletic Advisory Board take to control spectator aggression.

Answers to Selected Chapter 23 Activities

Activity 23.1:   Defining Aggression

1. A (Although the hit was legal, the intent was to inflict harm.)

2. N (There was no intent to inflict harm.)

3. N (The action was not directed at another living being.)

4. A (Although the athlete felt she was hit first, her intent was to inflict harm.)

5. N (Although the other driver was killed, there was no intent to harm.)

6. A (Although many would consider this a tactically smart move, the intent was to inflict psychological harm in the form of fear and anxiety to another.)

7. A (As in question 6, the intent was to inflict psychological harm.)

8. N (Although harm resulted, there was no intent to harm.)

Activity 23.2:   Recognizing When Aggression Is Most Likely to Occur

1. Aggression is most likely to occur when people experience failure, goal blockage (are losing), are embarrassed, perceive unfair officiating, are physically in pain, or are playing below their capabilities.

2. Because those that act aggressively have learned that aggression is a socially acceptable or appropriate response, and those who don't have learned that aggression is not socially acceptable or appropriate.

3. Previous reinforcement (or a lack of punishment) for aggressive responses in similar situations and the observations of high status athletes being rewarded for similar behaviors.

Activity 23.3:   Controlling Spectator Aggression

1. Develop strict alcohol-control policies and enforce them (e.g., check all backpacks to make sure nothing is brought into venues and hire extra security to monitor areas outside the buildings to ensure the no-alcohol policy).

2. Penalize spectators (e.g., kick them out) immediately for aggressive acts. Stop aggression as soon as it starts and inform other spectators it will not be tolerated.

3. When hiring officials, request people whom you know won't tolerate aggression on the field.

4. Inform coaches that aggressive displays on their part will not be tolerated.

5. Work with the media to convey the importance of not glorifying aggressive acts in sports coverage.

6. Develop a peer conflict-resolution program for all students.

7. Educate police and security officials on the causes of aggression in sport.

24

Character Development and Sportspersonship

concepts

- Character development and sportspersonship concern morality in sport and physical activity; that is, they are our views and actions about what is right or ethical and wrong or unethical in sport and physical activity settings. Character encompasses four interrelated values: compassion, fairness, sportspersonship, and integrity.

- There are three views as to how character and sportspersonship develop in athletes. The social learning approach emphasizes modeling, reinforcement, and social comparison. The structural-developmental approach contends that moral reasoning is related to a person's level of cognitive development. The social-psychological approach combines the first two approaches and suggests that a complex person-by-situation perspective determines character development and sportspersonship.

- Moral reasoning and moral behavior are linked by a moral-action process that includes four stages: interpreting the situation as one that involves some moral judgement, deciding on the best course of action, making a choice to act morally, and implementing a moral response.

- Strategies for developing character and sportspersonship include: defining what you consider sportspersonship in precise terms; reinforcing and encouraging sportspersonlike behaviors, and penalizing and discouraging unsportspersonlike behaviors; conveying rationales; emphasizing why actions are appropriate or inappropriate, the intent of actions, role-taking, compassion, and empathy; discussing moral dilemmas; building moral dilemmas and choices into practice and class contexts; teaching cooperative learning strategies; engineering task-oriented, motivational climates; and transferring power from leaders to participants.

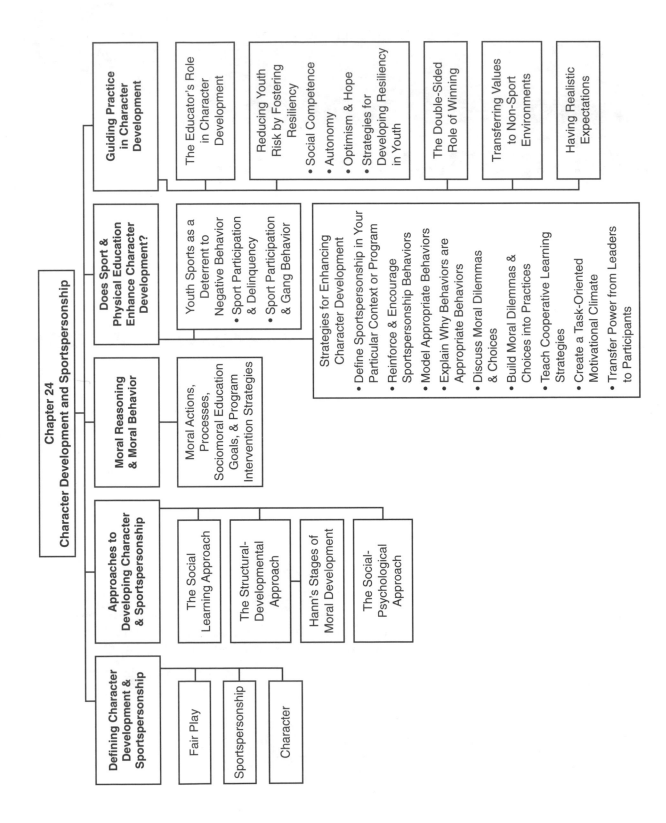

Chapter 24
Character Development and Sportspersonship

Defining Character Development & Sportspersonship
- Fair Play
- Sportspersonship
- Character

Approaches to Developing Character & Sportspersonship
- The Social Learning Approach
- The Structural-Developmental Approach
- Hann's Stages of Moral Development
- The Social-Psychological Approach

Moral Reasoning & Moral Behavior
- Moral Actions, Processes, Sociomoral Education Goals, & Program Intervention Strategies

Does Sport & Physical Education Enhance Character Development?
- Youth Sports as a Deterrent to Negative Behavior
  - Sport Participation & Delinquency
  - Sport Participation & Gang Behavior
- Strategies for Enhancing Character Development
  - Define Sportspersonship in Your Particular Context or Program
  - Reinforce & Encourage Sportspersonship Behaviors
  - Model Appropriate Behaviors
  - Explain Why Behaviors are Appropriate Behaviors
  - Discuss Moral Dilemmas & Choices
  - Build Moral Dilemmas & Choices into Practices
  - Teach Cooperative Learning Strategies
  - Create a Task-Oriented Motivational Climate
  - Transfer Power from Leaders to Participants

Guiding Practice in Character Development
- The Educator's Role in Character Development
- Reducing Youth Risk by Fostering Resiliency
  - Social Competence
  - Autonomy
  - Optimism & Hope
  - Strategies for Developing Resiliency in Youth
- The Double-Sided Role of Winning
- Transferring Values to Non-Sport Environments
- Having Realistic Expectations

- Some philosophically oriented issues to consider in facilitating character development are the educator's role in character development, the double-sided role of winning, transferring values to non-sport environments, and maintaining realistic expectations of the character-development process. Physical activity specialists also play an important role in fostering resiliency in underserved youth.

Activity 24.1

Defining Sportspersonship

Do this activity after reading chapter 24 of *Foundations of Sport and Exercise Psychology*.

Directions: Think about a sport you participated in (e.g., baseball, volleyball), and identify the level at which you participated (e.g., little league, high school, college). Then indicate what sportspersonship means in that sport. Be detailed and specific in your definition.

Sport: _____

Level played: _____

1. In this sport, sportspersonship is:

2. Would your definition of sportspersonship be the same for those involved in beginning youth, middle school, high school, college, and professional levels of your sport?

3. Why?

Activity 24.2

Understanding Fair Play, Sportspersonship, and Character

Do this activity after reading chapter 24 of *Foundations of Sport and Exercise Psychology*.

Directions: Respond to the following questions.

1. Define the following terms.

   Fair play:

   Sportspersonship:

   Character:

Compassion:

Integrity:

2. Now make a drawing that visually shows the relationship between these concepts.

You Make the Call:
Judging Appropriate Behavior in Sport

Do this activity after reading chapter 24 of *Foundations of Sport and Exercise Psychology.*

Directions: Think about the following sport situations and indicate whether you feel they are appropriate or inappropriate actions. Specify why.

1. You are a player on a baseball team and the opposing pitcher intentionally throws at your teammates. Would you retaliate by throwing at him or her? Why or why not?

2. You are a professional ice hockey coach. Is it appropriate to have one of your players assigned to constantly check the other team's "star" player in hopes of frustrating him and getting him in a fight—and thus placed in the penalty box?

3. You are in a tennis match and your opponent has consistently cheated on line calls, calling the ball out when it was clearly in. Should you cheat on his line calls in an effort to stop him from doing so?

> **Activity 24.4**

Enhancing Character Development and Sportspersonship

Do this activity after reading chapter 24 of *Foundations of Sport and Exercise Psychology.*

Directions: You have assumed a position as a volunteer youth soccer coach of boys and girls from ages 9 to 12. While the league's organizers are interested in skill development and fun, their charter mandates that character development and sportspersonship are the primary goals of participation. Based on what you have learned in this unit, use the following strategies to achieve this objective.

1. Define *sportspersonship.* Be specific.

2. How would you use reinforcement and penalties to achieve your objective?

3. How would you use models to achieve your objective?

4. How could rationales be employed?

5. In what ways would you integrate discussions of moral dilemmas?

6. How would you build moral dilemmas and choices into practices and games?

Answers to Selected Chapter 24 Activities

Activity 24.2: Understanding Fair Play, Sportspersonship, and Character

1. *Fair play:* When all contestants understand and adhere not only to the formal rules of the game but also to the spirit of cooperation and unwritten rules of play necessary to ensure that a contest is fair.

   Sportspersonship: An intense striving to succeed, tempered by commitment to the play spirit such that ethical standards will take precedence over strategic gain when the two conflict.

   Character: An array of characteristics (usually connoting a positive moral overtone such as developing self-control and persistence) that can be developed in sport

   Compassion: The ability to take on and appreciate the feelings of others—it is related to empathy.

   Integrity: The ability to maintain one's morality and fairness coupled with the belief that one can (and will) fulfill one's moral intentions.

2.

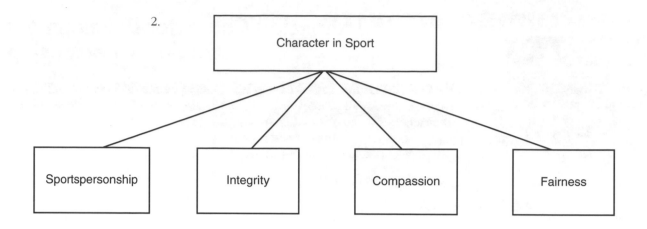

CONCLUDING ACTIVITY

Why Study Sport and Exercise Psychology?

Do this activity after completing *Foundations of Sport and Exercise Psychology.*

Directions: Select one of the following scenarios for group discussion. In your group, derive a group response to the posed situation and summarize it on a separate sheet of paper. See how your response compares to the points listed on the next page.

Scenario 1: Athletic Trainer—Mary Jo, the head athletic trainer at Campbell State College, has been working with Campbell's star running back, Kevin Jones, who is recovering from knee surgery. Kevin has made tremendous progress over the spring and summer and has achieved a 99% physical recovery. The coaches, however, have noticed that Kevin still favors his formerly injured knee in practice and is very hesitant when making cutbacks. Mary Jo knows that Kevin has physically recovered, but she's not sure how to help him regain his former confidence.

Scenario 2: Coach—Jeff is the point guard on the high school basketball team that you coach. For your team to repeat as league champions, Jeff needs to play well, especially in clutch situations. However, you have learned from coaching Jeff last season that he becomes very nervous in competition. In fact, the bigger the game or the more critical the situation, the more nervous Jeff becomes and the worse he plays. Your biggest coaching challenge this season will be helping Jeff learn to manage stress.

Scenario 3: Fitness Leader—Sally is serving in her second year as fitness director for the St. Peters Hospital Cardiac Rehabilitation Program. She spent countless hours in her first year organizing and initiating her aerobic fitness program for individuals recovering from cardiac arrest. The program was very well received by both the patients and hospital administration. Recently, however, Sally has become concerned about a very high lack of adherence on the part of her clients. They just don't seem to stick with their exercise programs after they start feeling better. As many as 60% are dropping out before they make exercise a lifelong habit. Sally must get her clients to adhere to their exercise regimes, but she doesn't know how. Problems like these were never discussed in her classes in exercise physiology or exercise program design for cardiac rehabilitation.

Scenario 4: Physical Educator—Bob has wanted to be a physical educator ever since he can remember. He is a student teacher this semester, and he is becoming increasingly frustrated. The high school students in his classes are totally out of shape and have no interest in learning lifelong sport skills and becoming physically fit. It is all Bob can do to get them to participate in the mild exercise program during their 40-minute classes held twice a week. Bob's goal for the semester is to get his sedentary students motivated to learn lifelong sport skills and engage in fitness activities.

Scenario 5: Sport Psychologist—Tom is a sport psychologist and long-time Chicago Cubs baseball fan. His dream consulting position has recently become available: The owners of the Cubs, frustrated by the lack of team cohesion, have asked Tom to submit a consulting proposal designed to improve team cohesion. Tom has a week to design a psychological skills training program to enhance team cohesion and, he hopes, secure his dream position as sport psychology consultant for the Chicago Cubs.

Note: There are a number of ways to address these five scenarios, so no one correct answer exists. Student responses, however, should reflect the content listed below.

Scenario 1: Athletic Trainer

- Check for signs of poor adjustment to injury (page 495 in text).
- Devise Sport Psychology injury rehabilitation programs with a special emphasis on social support (pages 405-409 in text).
- Implement anxiety-reduction techniques (pages 248-256 in text).
- Design a goal-setting program (pages 318-322 in text).
- Use shaping to reinforce use of recovered leg (pages 119, 124-128 in text).

Scenario 2: Coach

- Understand the situation by applying the stress process and understanding how arousal affects performance (pages 74-90 in text).
- Implement a psychological skills training program (pages 223-224 in text) focusing on arousal regulation strategies (pages 245-263 in text).
- Understand that imagery (pages 265-284 in text), self-confidence (pages 285-304 in text), and concentration (pages 325-350 in text) are relevant.

Scenario 3: Fitness Leader

- Understand reasons for (and not for) exercising (pages 372-375 in text).
- Focus on implementing strategies for enhancing exercise adherence (pages 384-392 in text).
- Understand that motivation (pages 47-70 in text); feedback and reinforcement, and intrinsic motivation principles (pages 115-172 in text); as well as goal-setting principles (pages 305-324) are also relevant.

Scenario 4: Physical Educator

- Make an effort to understand and enhance motivation (pages 47-70 in text).
- Understand that feedback and reinforcement, and intrinsic motivation principles (pages 115-172 in text), as well as goal-setting principles (pages 305-324 in text) are relevant.
- Understand reasons for (and not for) exercising (pages 372-375 in text).
- Focus on implementing strategies for enhancing exercise adherence (pages 384-392 in text).

Scenario 5: Sport Psychologist

- Implement a psychological skills training program (pages 223-244 in text).
- Pay special attention to understanding group and team dynamics and group cohesion (pages 145-186 in text).
- Understand that guidelines for enhancing cohesion are especially relevant (pages 179-184 in text).

REFERENCES

American Coaching Effectiveness program. (1987) *Sport Psychology*, Level Two. Champaign, IL: Human Kinetics.

Carron, A.V., Brawley, L.R., & Widmeyer, W.N. (1985). *Group environment questionnaire*. London, Ontario: Sports Dynamics.

Gould, D., Ruffey, S., Vory, E., & Loehr, J. (1996). Burnout in competitive junior tennis players: A quantitative psychological assessment. *The Sport Psychologist, 10*, 322-340.

Martens, R. (1990). *Coaches guide to sport psychology*. Champaign, IL: Human Kinetics.

Martens, R., Vealey, R.S., & Burton, D. (1990). *Competitive anxiety in sport*. Champaign, IL: Human Kinetics.

Martin, F. & Lumsden, J. (1987). *Coaching: An effective behavioral approach*. St. Louis: Times Mirror/Mosby.

Orlick, T. (1986). *Psyching for sport*. Champaign, IL: Human Kinetics.

Smith, R.E., Schultz, R.W., Smoll, F.L., & Ptacek, J.T. (1994). Development and validation of a multi-dimensional measure of sport-specific psychological skills: The Athletic Coping Skills Inventory. *Journal of Sport and Exercise Psychology, 17*, 379-398.

Smith, R.E., Smoll, F.L., & Schultz, R.W. (1990). Measurement and correlates of sport-specific cognitive and somatic trait anxiety: The Sport Anxiety Scale. *Anxiety Research, 2*, 263-280.

Vealey, R.S. (1986). Conceptualization of sport-confidence and competitive orientation: Preliminary investigation and instrument development. *Journal of Sport Psychology, 8*, 221-246.